T0330660

The Economics of Libraries

Libraries are included in the widely accepted definition of Cultural and Creative Industries, together with heritage, performing arts, museums, visual arts, and archives, and they play an important role in the creative value chain. *The Economics of Libraries* highlights the economic importance of the library sector.

Providing an accessible and concise expert overview of the most important economic features and diversified functions of libraries, the authors also summarise the challenges and opportunities deriving from digital technologies, the management of cultural infrastructures, and audience development. This unique short-form book fills a longstanding gap in our understanding of the demand and supply of library services.

This book will be of interest to researchers and scholars in the fields of economics and the creative and cultural industries. It also provides useful insights for students and lecturers, as well as topics of discussion for professionals.

Marco Ferdinando Martorana is Senior Assistant Professor of Public Economics at the University of Catania, Italy.

Ilde Rizzo is Professor of Public Economics at the University of Catania, Italy.

Routledge Research in the Creative and Cultural Industries

Series Editor: Ruth Rentschler

This series brings together book-length original research in cultural and creative industries from a range of perspectives. Charting developments in contemporary cultural and creative industries' thinking around the world, the series aims to shape the research agenda to reflect the expanding significance of the creative sector in a globalised world.

Digital Transformation in the Recording Industry
Evolution of Power: From The Turntable To Blockchain
Anna Anetta Janowska

Diversity and Inclusion: Are We Nearly There Yet?
Target Setting in the Screen Industries
Doris Ruth Eikhof

Creative Work
Conditions, Contexts and Practices
*Edited by Erika Andersson Cederholm, Katja Lindqvist,
Ida de Wit Sandström and Philip Warkander*

Data-Driven Innovation in the Creative Industries
*Edited by Melissa Terras, Vikki Jones, Nicola Osborne and
Chris Speed*

The Economics of Libraries
Marco Ferdinando Martorana and Ilde Rizzo

For more information about this series, please visit: www.routledge.com/Routledge-Research-in-the-Creative-and-Cultural-Industries/book-series/RRCCI

The Economics of Libraries

**Marco Ferdinando Martorana
and Ilde Rizzo**

Routledge
Taylor & Francis Group

LONDON AND NEW YORK

First published 2024
by Routledge
4 Park Square, Milton Park, Abingdon, Oxon OX14 4RN

and by Routledge
605 Third Avenue, New York, NY 10158

Routledge is an imprint of the Taylor & Francis Group, an informa business

British Library Cataloguing-in-Publication Data
A catalogue record for this book is available from the British Library

ISBN: 9781032364278 (hbk)
ISBN: 9781032364285 (pbk)
ISBN: 9781003331896 (ebk)

DOI: 10.4324/9781003331896

Typeset in Times New Roman
by Newgen Publishing UK

Contents

1 Introduction

Libraries are cultural institutions with a very long history, somehow parallel to the history of the accumulation and transmission of knowledge through writing, their longevity reflecting a vital function in social organizations (Salaün, 2013). The historical perspective of libraries is outside the scope of this book. However, it is worth noting that libraries have gradually diversified their functions over time and have been careful to adapt to the new media and new cultural industries, also being very permeable to technical change.

Nowadays, libraries are widespread around the world and serve a very high number of users. In fact, according to the International Federation of Library Associations and Institutions' (IFLA) 'Library Map of the World' (LMW, henceforth),[1] about 2.8 million libraries are currently open over the globe, employing more than 2 million workers and volunteers, serving more than a billion registered users in 2022, for a total of more than 5 billion physical visits, loaning almost 8 billion physical volumes and more than 14 billion electronic volumes.

Notwithstanding these impressive data and the wide range of the related socio-economic effects, libraries have been almost disregarded by cultural economists as a subject of systematic analysis, especially if compared with other cultural organizations such as museums. This is probably because the economic role of libraries is not immediately visible nor readily measurable. On the contrary, the large number of studies in Library Information Science and Library management are mainly concerned with the evaluation of libraries' economic value, with advocacy purposes (Salaün, 2013).

In very general terms, libraries can be considered part of the so-called Cultural and Creative Industries (CCI), a segment of the

DOI: 10.4324/9781003331896-1

economy that has gained increasing attention since the 1990s, referring to

> all cultural and creative sectors whose activities are based on cul-
> tural values and/or artistic and other creative expressions, whether
> those activities are market- or non-market-oriented, whatever the
> type of structure that carries them out, and irrespective of how that
> structure is financed.
>
> (EIF, 2019, p. 9)

CCI have been investigated, following different models and leading
to different definitions (Towse, 2020; OECD, 2022). CCI studies
emphasize the links between culture, creativity and economic growth
and development.[2] Indeed, libraries are included in most definitions
of CCI; for instance, the United Nations Conference on Trade and
Development (UNCTAD) (2010) classification of Creative Industries,
considers libraries as a sub-group of Heritage.[3] Similarly, libraries
are at the core of the European Union definition that places them in
a subsector of Heritage, together with archaeological sites, archives,
and museums (Kea, 2006).[4] Conceptual and definitional issues imply
different measures across countries (Bakhshi, 2020). However, a
common tenet is that Heritage contribution to the production of cultural content, creativity, and innovation is crucial, even though its
share of CCI value added, employment, and number of companies is
relatively small (EIF, 2019).

Within such a broad framework, the present book is building upon
a wide multidisciplinary literature and investigates, from an economic
point of view, the libraries' activities and their relationship with the
society and economy. Chapter 2 analyses the different typologies of
libraries – public, private, academic, national, school and so forth – and
their related variegated functions, focusing on their economic features,
ranging from private divisible services to public goods – and the
implications for the functioning of the market and the role of public
sector. Attention is also devoted to the effects on the economy and the
related valuation issues. Chapters 3 and 4, respectively, investigate the
supply and demand of library services, considering the analogies with
other cultural institutions, while stressing libraries' own peculiarities.
More precisely, Chapter 3 explores the most relevant issues regarding
the provision of library services – identifying the relevant inputs and
outputs as well as the factors that affect such provision – and discusses

efficiency issues and organizational models. Chapter 4 highlights the key theoretical economic issues related to market and non-market demand for library services as well as the drivers of cultural participation, providing also some European and North American data. The effects of technology on the demand and supply of library services are investigated in Chapter 5, taking into account the differences across cultural organizations and their business models as well as the challenges posed by the COVID-19 pandemic. Some empirical evidence drawn from European and North American surveys is also provided. Finally, Chapter 6 offers brief concluding remarks.

Notes

1 https://librarymap.ifla.org
2 For an overview of the evolution of the concepts of CCI and of their various definitions, see Dalle Nogare & Murzyn-Kupisz (2021). The literature on CCI is very extensive (O'Connor, 2010); a bibliometric analysis, has been recently provided by Bui Hoai et al. (2021).
3 Libraries are part of the sub-sector Cultural Sites (together with Archaeological Sites, Museums and Exhibitions), the other sub-sector of Heritage being Traditional Cultural Expressions. The other three groups of activities and related sub-sectors considered in the UNCTAD classification are Arts (Visual arts and Performing arts), Media (Publishing and printed books and Audiovisuals) and Functional Creations (Design, New Media and Creative Services).
4 The Kea definition follows the concentric circles model with the proportion of cultural to commercial content decreasing from the centre outwards. The core arts field, that is, the inner Circle, includes, in addition to Heritage, two other sectors (Visual Arts and Performing Arts). Cultural Industries, that is, the Circle 1, include Film and Video, Videogames, Broadcasting, Music, Book and Press while Design, Architecture and Advertising are part of the Creative Industries (Circle 2).

References

Bakhshi, H. (2020). Measuring the creative economy. In Bille, T., Mignosa, A. & Towse, R. (Eds.). *Teaching cultural economics*. Cheltenham: Edward Elgar Publishing, 230–237.

Bui Hoai, S., Hoang Thi, B., Nguyen Lan, P., & Tran, T. (2021). A bibliometric analysis of cultural and creative industries in the field of arts and humanities. *Digital Creativity*, 32(4), 307–322. https://doi.org/10.1080/14626268.2021.1993928

Dalle Nogare, C., & Murzyn-Kupisz, M. (2021). Do museums foster innovation through engagement with the cultural and creative industries? *Journal of Cultural Economics*, 45, 671–704. https://doi.org/10.1007/s10 824-021-09418-3

EIF (European Investment Fund) (2019). *Market analysis of the cultural and creative sectors in Europe* www.eif.org/what_we_do/guarantees/cultural_ creative_sectors_guarantee_facility/ccs-market-analysis-europe.pdf

KEA European Affairs (2006). *The Economy of Culture in Europe*, Study for the European Commission, DG Education and Culture. https://ec.europa. eu/assets/eac/culture/library/studies/cultural-economy_en.pdf

O'Connor, J. (2010). *The cultural and creative industries: A literature review*, 2nd ed., Creativity, Culture and Education Series. Literature_review_ second_edition.pdf (qut.edu.au)

OECD (2022). *The culture fix. Creative people, places and industries*, Local Economic and Employment Development (LEED). Paris: OECD Publishing. https://doi.org/10.1787/991bb520-en

Salaün, J. M. (2013). The immeasurable economics of libraries. In Rizzo, I. & Mignosa, A. (Eds.). *Handbook on the economics of cultural heritage*, Cheltenham: Edward Elgar Publishing, 480–507.

Towse, R. (2020). Creative industries. In Towse, R. & Navarrete Hernández, T. (Eds.). *Handbook of cultural economics*, 3rd ed., Cheltenham: Edward Elgar Publishing, 137–144.

UNCTAD (2010). *Creative economy. Report 2010*. Geneva: UNCTAD. https://unctad.org/system/files/official-document/ditctab20103_en.pdf

2   The Economics of Libraries

General Issues

2.1 Introduction

Libraries are probably the most widespread cultural institutions, and can be considered part of any urban landscape, being located in big towns as well as in small cities and villages.

What is a library? What is its mission? Though these questions may seem apparently trivial, the answers are not straightforward. In fact, libraries are quite heterogeneous entities as far as size, content, and institutional organization are concerned, evolving through time in line with societal and technological changes.

In very general terms, libraries are productive entities, providing a wide range of socially valuable cultural services, and such a contribution to society needs to be assessed to take into account their heterogeneity. Moreover, library services are not easily characterized from the economic perspective, because of the absence of a market and, thus, of a reliable measure of the individual willingness to pay (WTP)[1] for their activities. In very simple terms, the services of libraries are denoted by two phases: assembling the collection and organizing the users' access to it. Following Salaün (2013, p. 489) 'the library is building an ecosystem of its own', in the sense that formerly scattered documents are brought together and are made available in one place for those who are interested, while at the same time libraries function as a network through the interlibrary loan of the items in the collection.

In this chapter, we try to disentangle such a complex sector, considering the different types of libraries in terms of content and institutional features (Section 2) and the functions related to the different typologies. In Section 3, we then investigate how the different types of libraries affect society's wellbeing, providing a

DOI: 10.4324/9781003331896-2

rationale for the role of the public sector at the various levels of government, and how public intervention takes place. Evaluation issues are discussed in Section 4. Finally, Section 5 provides an overview of the funding issues.

2.2 Types of Libraries and Related Functions

2.2.1 Classification

Libraries are heterogeneous organizations, and their classification is not straightforward. The IFLS Library Map of the World (IFLA LMW)[2] classifies libraries in six categories, namely, National, Academic, Public, Community, School, and Other, with a prominent presence of School and Public libraries.[3]

According to such classification, National libraries are those collecting documents published in a specific country; Academic are those whose primary function is supporting learning and research (thus including university and research libraries); Public libraries are non-profit libraries open to the general public and usually financed by the public sector; Community libraries are those out a statutory library provision and are not managed by National or local authorities; School libraries are those attached to schools. The residual category, 'Other', may still include public libraries, such as government libraries, jointly with private libraries, such as the industrial ones.

On the one hand, such classification overlaps ownership, source of funding and functions. For instance, public funding pertains not only to public libraries but also characterizes other types, or the school libraries, provided that schools are often public entities, too. From an economic perspective, public funding or subsidization of libraries is grounded on the economic features of library services or on equity issues.[4] On the other hand, what differentiates the above types is the size, in terms of collected items and number of users, the latter having broadly different motivations – for example, motivations from leisure to research – although overlapping still occurs.[5] Moreover, regardless of the above different types, in analogy with heritage (Rizzo, 2023), a distinction can be drawn, depending on quality – for instance, between worldwide known libraries versus regional or local libraries and between libraries located within an urban environment and those located outside – although the latter aspect, because of the characteristics of libraries services, is not likely to occur as frequently as for heritage.[6]

2.2.2 Functions

Libraries fulfil a range of functions, with differences among types, although some of them are common to all. The first function carried out by libraries is the collection of items in accordance with the library's function, leading to the huge collections of national libraries as well as to the minor ones in small community libraries or to the highly specialized ones. It is however worth noting that, as a consequence of digital technologies, collections have changed their features, including e-books, e-journals and, more in general digital resources, whose 'weight' is increasing through time,[7] alongside print-on-paper resources. Salaün (2013) points out some peculiar features in the size and composition of collections: consultations tend to take into consideration only a very limited number of documents, while the great majority of documents are rarely demanded.[8] However, in line with their mission, the items are kept in the collection to increase the potential of the library for readers over time.[9] A peculiar feature of many libraries, however, is to be part of a network (Salaün, 2013). A well-known example is that operating in the United Kingdom, based on a main library and several outlets, sometimes supported by additional mobile libraries, aimed at serving a large area (Hammond, 2002).

Indeed, the conservation of collections is a basic function of libraries, which may imply different production processes and organizations depending on the specific nature of the collection, ranging from the restoration of valuable old items to the conservation of digital resources. Anyway, conservation allows for the transmission of information gathered over time.

The cataloguing of library materials is also a crucial function required to make collections accessible and allow for their effective use. To this end referencing and lending services are necessary. Lending printed books is the library service that appears to be used most (OCLC, 2005) worldwide[10]; despite the marked digitization trend of collections and borrowing, in the US libraries in the last 15 years, physical items like books and magazines are still borrowed the most, though with a declining trend (Rizzo, 2022).[11] Referencing is a crucial tool to allow the reader to save time in finding the document or the information she is looking for. Librarians as 'translators and coaches' (for academic libraries, Fister, 2009) play a major role, though libraries automation tools are likely to empower users.[12]

However, *mutatis mutandis,* the role of librarians appears more pervasive and is crucial to support users compared with the staffs of museums or other cultural institutions, because of the differences in the type of the service provided.

How collections are actually accessed and used, whether physically – through loan services or reading on site – or online – through digital access services and sharing digitized items–[13] very much depends on many factors such as, for instance, on the item's characteristics, on the type of users and their motivation, as well as on libraries' organization and physical features. Thus, the open question is whether and how libraries need to be reinvented to still remain 'a place' (Bennet et al., 2005).[14]

Alongside the above-mentioned basic functions, most libraries perform other and diversified functions,[15] such as being a place for training courses, providing access terminals to the Internet, organizing activities for children, promoting programmes for creating and exhibiting artwork or, more generally, offering an area for the local community to use (Del Barrio et al., 2021).[16] The coexistence of these additional functions with the basic functions and their combination cannot be taken for granted, since they vary across types of libraries and depend on their specific features and on related incentives facing the library's management and staff as well as on the socio-economic conditions of the area where libraries are located. Differences also occur across countries, depending on their economic status and on the stance of cultural policy (public spending, legislation, etc.).

The varied nature of libraries is well captured in the Manifesto issued by IFLA and UNESCO (2022), updating the 1994 Manifesto, referring to public libraries:

> The public library is the local centre of information, making all kinds of knowledge and information readily available to its users. It is an essential component of knowledge societies, continuously adapting to new means of communication to fulfil their mandate of providing universal access to and enabling meaningful use of information for all people. It provides publicly accessible space for the production of knowledge, sharing and exchange of information and culture, and promotion of civic engagement.
>
> 2022 IFLA-UNESCO (p. 1)

According to the Manifesto, the key missions of public libraries relate to information, literacy, education, inclusivity, civic participation and culture. 'Through these key missions, public libraries contribute to the Sustainable Development Goals and the construction of more equitable, humane, and sustainable societies' (p. 2). In other words, libraries are assigned a prominent role for promoting society's well-being and as institutions underpinning democracy and contributing to building communities. It is worth noting that the acknowledgement of the changing and expanding role of libraries in the contemporary knowledge society,[17] as represented by the above mentioned 2022 Manifesto, has characterized other cultural institutions. This is the case, of museums, as witnessed by the new International Council of Museums (ICOM) definition, aimed at representing the major changes in the role of museums today (Seymour, 2022).

It is widely agreed that a major issue regarding public libraries that is common to those receiving public support, is the capability of communicating their value – that is, their contribution to society – to a wide range of decision makers, stakeholders, and non-users to motivate (if not to legitimate) public support, especially in an era of public budget cuts (Halpin et al., 2015).[18] Yet, as a survey carried out on six European countries[19] shows, the three legitimations for supporting libraries that come highest in the ranking, are their roles as cultural heritage institutions, as providers of equal access to knowledge and literature and as places for learning. Being a community meeting place and an arena for public debate are ranked in last place in all six countries (Audunson et al., 2019).

The above statement regarding public libraries, being, on the one hand, very wide, does not pertain to all types of libraries, for instance to private or specialized libraries that are not likely to consider civic engagement among their objectives. On the other hand, it is not exhaustive, since other specific missions characterize other types of libraries: for instance, supporting research is at the core of academic libraries.

It is also worth mentioning that in the cultural economics literature the importance of heritage to promote cultural tourism[20] is usually emphasized for museums, immovable cultural heritage, and intangible cultural heritage while the role of libraries is rarely considered. And, yet, it may be important also for libraries, library tourism being, however, an old phenomenon (Kells, 2019), which nowadays exhibits marked and increasing potentialities. These potentialities pertain to different types of libraries worldwide,[21] located in buildings of historical or architectural importance, having specialized collections or outstanding and unique items,[22] or being related to other tangible and intangible heritages in the area.[23] To what extent these potentialities are captured and exploited may be constrained by the lack of the needed specific skills of library staff and also by other factors, such as existing cultural policies, a necessary requirement being strong collaboration among different cultural institutions (Bovero, 2009).

2.3 Normative and Positive Issues of Government Intervention

2.3.1 Market Failure and Normative Motivations for Government Intervention

As outlined above, the different types of libraries provide different services, giving rise to a wide range of effects on individuals as well as on society as a whole. Many actors are involved, generating different economic implications.

As for heritage (Peacock, 1997), *mutatis mutandis,* libraries can be considered to be a capital asset, with at least two different dimensions: a physical one, implying the allocation of resources for the increase and /or the conservation of collections,[24] and another dimension consisting in a flow of services offered by libraries to be consumed, or to be used for production purposes[25] or not necessarily related to the use but only to their existence, in the present as well as in the future.

Several economic arguments about the significance of cultural heritage to society imply 'market failure' and provide a rationale for government intervention (Borowiecki et al., 2023). More precisely, markets 'fail' because of public goods, externalities, and non-use benefits, such as option, bequest and existence benefits.[26] In all these cases the market price mechanism is not able to allocate resources efficiently, because the above benefits are not reflected by the price,[27] and the challenge of valuing cultural output arises.[28] Moreover, equity issues, in terms of accessibility also arise. The same arguments apply to libraries, though with different weights, depending on their specific features.

Several examples can be put forward for 'market failure' in the library field. Some activities, such as the conservation of the items of historical and artistic values in the collection and the archival function allowing for the transmission to future generations of heritage and memories, exhibit public goods characteristics, being non-excludable and non-rival. To a greater extent, externalities occur both in production and consumption even if library activities and services are excludable. For instance, using a library may have positive effects not only on the user but also on social welfare with important economic implications. In fact, libraries provide positive effects on education (Clark & Hawkins, 2011), human and cultural capital accumulation (Leguina et al., 2021), social capital accumulation (Vårheim et al., 2008; Vårheim, 2014) and health (Philbin et al., 2019).[29] Moreover, libraries reduce inequality, being places for learning and empowerment for those lacking opportunities at home, allowing for democratic access to information and knowledge and reducing the digital divide, providing hardware, software, and Internet connection (Leguina et al., 2021).[30] Libraries are also found to be important in equalizing social and economic differences, acting as a meeting place and providing possibilities of being an active citizen (Aabø et al., 2010).

In addition to the above social and educational benefits, libraries may generate different positive effects on the local economy depending on their specific features (Arts Council England, 2014): for instance, a library located in an outstanding building of sufficient scale and interest can play a role in urban regeneration programs, enhancing the image of the area and contributing to attract visitors. Moreover, a further contribution to local economic development may be exerted, providing added value information and supporting business and enterprises, especially the small and medium ones, through specialist library services (Dos Santos, 2009).[31]

The positive impacts of the above benefits of libraries on local communities' resilience (Vårheim, 2017), on the economy (Skelly et al., 2015), and local development (Manjarrez et al., 2007; Arts Council England, 2014)[32] are widely acknowledged, though no causality assessment is provided.[33]

The above arguments about the relevance of libraries for society's welfare are just some examples of the benefits that cannot be provided through the market, since they are not reflected by the price mechanism and call for public action to avoid their under-provision, in accord with individuals' preferences. Public intervention is also motivated because of equity reasons to increase accessibility, foster social inclusion, and reduce social and economic barriers.

2.3.2 Features of the Public Decision-making Process

Moving from a normative to a positive perspective, it is worth noting that while the existence of market failure is widely agreed upon, government action is criticized, claiming that it is subject to failure – the so called 'public failure' – and does not necessarily ensure efficiency (Frey, 2020; Towse, 2019). Almost everywhere in the heritage field the government has a prominent role, though with different quantitative and qualitative features. Differences pertain to the amount of public resources, the mix of public tools, the institutional approaches, with effects also on the role played by the private and non-profit sectors.[34]

Thus, to analyse how public action operates in practice in the heritage field, the political economy perspective is increasingly adopted to investigate the public decision-making process (Mazza, 2020) and the negotiations taking place among several actors – policymakers, public officials/experts, providers of heritage services, organized groups with vested interests, and the general public. Cultural heritage policy decisions occur in a complex system of principal–agent relationships,[35] characterized by information asymmetry. A prominent role is played by experts, whose professional training influences the decisions regarding the allocation of resources and, therefore, the priorities of the decision-making process – that is, what heritage to conserve/supply and how – and enhances their status. In some circumstances, also depending on the legal and administrative framework, a 'custodianship' model, limiting the access to heritage and its use may prevail (OECD, 2018). Therefore, an open crucial question is whether public decisions represent the preference of the public (Peacock, 1994). If decisions are taken 'top-down', the values of elite or dominant groups tend to prevail, and the role of heritage as a tool to promote cultural participation and social inclusion is greatly weakened (Mignosa, 2016). It is a common tenet, however, that the level of public participation in the decision-making can be improved by political devolution, being the link between heritage and local communities particularly strong (Martorana et al., 2019).[36]

No specific attention has been paid to apply the political economy perspective to libraries, but similar arguments hold, though with some differences related to their specific features. Indeed, notwithstanding the analogies in the functioning of the public decision-making process, it is worth noting that the role of expertise seems a bit different. It appears rather similar only for specific types of libraries, such as those

with historical or highly specialized collections because of the specificity of the knowledge and expertise required to evaluate the quality
of the items and the issues of their preservation. In all the other cases,
that is, in the majority of libraries, the identification as well as the
features of the profession are less straightforward – librarians qualify
themselves as 'information professionals' – as well the applicability
of the concept of expertise as such (Stover, 2004). A major difference
is that the relationship of librarians with the library users is closer than
in other cultural fields, such as museums; in fact, librarians provide
a customized divisible service to meet the individual users' demand
for information.[37] Following Stover (2004, p. 12), the relationship
of librarians with users consists of three kinds of assistance: 'bibliographical assistance (finding a book or document in the library or outside the library); question answering (finding the answer to a specific,
fact-based question); and selection assistance (recommending a book
for a specific purpose)'.

2.3.3 Role of Librarians

It is outside the scope of this work to deal with the longstanding
debate on the duties of librarians toward their patrons (Weckert &
Ferguson, 1993), a crucial issue being to what extent librarians should
answer or not all users' requests of information.[38] More recently, new
challenges have arisen: the so-called right to be forgotten, which
alters the norms of information flow in libraries (Kritikos, 2018)
and the implementation of Artificial Intelligence, which implies to
balance the efficiency in the access to information with its equity and
inclusiveness (Subaveerapandiyan, 2023).To what extent librarians
interact with customers on a peer-to-peer basis or use a technical
jargon to enhance their stance of experts – making difficult the interaction with customers – depends on many factors, such as the kind of
library, its institutional features and the related incentives librarians
face in terms of effective and efficient performance. On the grounds
of the above considerations, however, it seems that in the case of
library, the decision-making process appears more demand-oriented
than in other heritage fields (with the exception of archives): library
services are mainly divisible, the relationship between library staff
and users is closer with a greater interaction than in other cultural
organizations and, therefore, a diffused bottom-up monitoring is
likely to take place.

2.4 Valuation Issues

2.4.1 Aims

Valuation is particularly important as a policy tool to support decision-making in the cultural field, especially when services are provided for free, as, for instance, is the case in the majority of libraries. In addition to the efficiency evaluation[39] – that is the assessment of the economic value (in monetary terms) of the wellbeing that society obtains from cultural assets – valuation can also be used to estimate effectiveness – for example, the capability of cultural activities to meet the goals of cultural organizations or, at higher level, the goals of cultural policies. For instance, the effectiveness of library provision is the extent to which libraries fulfil their social purposes, and affect social outcomes, such as students' achievements and research outputs – in the case of school and university libraries (Chen, 1997) – cultural and social capital accumulation, reduction of inequality, and so forth. Evaluating effectiveness is generally a challenging task because objectives are usually multiple and rather vaguely stated, and the problem of identifying the causal effect is difficult to solve.

2.4.2 Methods

A very extensive academic literature and several official reports deal with the valuation of the contribution of cultural organizations to society's wellbeing (Wright & Eppink, 2016; Eftec, 2005). Different approaches are used, ranging from impact studies – assessing ex-ante economic effects, favoured by 'art people' (Frey 2005) and widely used as advocacy for libraries (Imholz & Arns, 2007; Arns et al., 2013) – to valuation studies, including several techniques such as Travel Cost, Hedonic Pricing, Contingent Valuation, Choice Experiment, and Subjective Wellbeing.[40] Once, non-market values are considered together with market values, a more comprehensive assessment of the libraries' contribution to social welfare is provided by Cost-Benefit Analysis[41] (see Box 2.1).

It is worth noting that economic valuation, estimating the values associated with cultural assets in monetary terms, raises peculiar issues in this field. In fact, as Throsby (2003, p. 279) outlines, the economic value 'comprises any direct use value of the cultural good or service in question, plus whatever non-market values it may give rise to.' It is, however, worth noting that in the cultural field economic and cultural values co-exist, and that the latter, being multidimensional,[42] with no single unit of account, can hardly be rendered in monetary terms,[43] leaving open the question of the relationship between economic and cultural values assessments in the individual's evaluation[44] (Throsby, 2012).

Box 2.1 Economic Valuation Methods

Impact studies aim at quantifying the overall economic effects on the economy generated by a cultural organization/library in terms of increased consumption, employment, and turnover. These total effects are measured considering not only the direct effects generated by the cultural institution but also the indirect – value generated across supply chains and visitor spending – and the induced ones – additional spending in the economy as a result of employment created (OECD, 2022). The latter reflects the interdependencies within the economy leading to multiplier effects, the rationale being that any injection of additional expenditure is likely to generate a multiplier effect, the size of which depends on interregional linkages (Bille, 2020). This approach is criticized by economists, however, because it disregards cultural, social and non-use values as well as cost opportunities, with the consequence that a misallocation of resources is likely to occur (Bille & Schulze, 2006; Seaman, 2020). Though, as Arts Council England (2014) outlines, such an approach is useful only for those libraries that are able to attract visitors from outside the area where the library is located.

Revealed preference and stated preference techniques can be used to assess the monetary value of non-market benefits associated with cultural assets (Provins et al., 2008).

Revealed preference approach attempts to infer use value from observed behaviour: Travel Cost (TC) and Hedonic Price (HP) being the most common methods.

TC uses information on visitors' time and cost of travel to and from a cultural site/library to estimate their WTP for the cultural/library services. Rather than valuing the site/library itself,

TC technically elicits the value of a trip to the site, and in multi-purpose trips it is difficult to disaggregate the value of a site (Lawton et al., 2020).

HP method analyses the property market to estimate indirectly the additional value for properties deriving from being near to cultural amenities. HP may be not well suited to value most cultural assets, which provide benefits to visitors but do not necessarily increase the price of houses nearby (Lawton et al., 2020).

Stated preference techniques can be used to estimate use and especially non-use values, the most common methods being Contingent Valuation (CV) and Choice Experiment (CE) (Snowball, 2013).

CV uses surveys to estimate individuals (users and/or non-users) WTP (e.g. in increased taxes or ticket prices) for hypothetical improvements in cultural/library services or their willingness to accept (WTA) for the cultural site/library deterioration or disappearance/closure. The individual evaluation is contingent to the scenarios described in the questionnaire and is also affected by the format of the questions, whether open-ended or close–ended, eliciting WTP and /or WTA.

A wide debate on CV stresses major challenges, such as hypothetical bias, differences between WTP and WTA, and lack of scope effects (Hausmann, 2012) and also provides some defense to the criticisms (Haab et al., 2013), with some scholars also suggesting that the WTP provided by CV studies might be biased (overestimated or underestimated) with respect to experimental or real-life markets, for instance, because of the presence of the warm glow effect (Lee et al., 2010), altruistic motivations (Lee & Chung, 2012), yea-saying bias (Blamey et al., 1999), pro-test answer (Fujiwara & Campbell, 2011) and information bias (Chung, 2008).

CE does not directly ask individuals their WTP, but instead proposes alternative combinations of the different attributes of cultural/library services, including price. Individuals choose between the proposed options, that is, between the 'bundles' of characteristics and the WTP for each attribute can be inferred indirectly. A possible shortcoming related to such a method is that survey respondents may be overburdened with an excessive number of attributes, with the risk of generating imprecise WTP values (Lawton et al., 2020).

Instead of asking people directly for their WTP, subjective wellbeing (SWB) considers people's self-reports of their own wellbeing as a measure of their welfare (Fujiwara, 2013). In some methodologies this effect of cultural engagement is expressed as a monetary value by estimating the amount of income that would result in an equivalent change in SWB. SWB questions may imply biases such as framing effects, order effects, time of interview and context bias (Lawton et al., 2020).

Cost-Benefit Analysis (CBA) is used (also in the library field – Elliott et al., 2007; Aabø, 2009; Tessler, 2013) to assess the effects of public decisions on social welfare, according to their net social benefit (i.e., the difference between benefits and costs) (Snowball, 2013). Use and non-use values associated with the cultural assets are quantified, for the former through market prices if available, or using revealed as well as stated preferences methods. Several issues are widely debated, such as the choice of the rate of discount (to compare the values of benefits and costs over time) or the consideration of equity issues through the introduction of weights.

2.5 Funding Issues

2.5.1 *Public Funding*

Libraries can rely on three sources of income: public funds from government, private donations, and their own resources. In general terms, there are similarities with other cultural institutions, such as museums, though there are peculiarities related to the specificity of libraries' activities. The composition of library funding, that is the 'weight' of these types of sources of income, is likely to vary depending on the type of library and on its size.

Official data on government funds refer to the wider cultural sector, with some differences depending on the source of data. According to Eurostat (2023), in 2021, general government[45] expenditure on cultural services[46] across the EU amounted to 71.2 billion euros, 0.5 percent of GDP or 1.0 percent of all general government expenditure, with marked differences across countries. Similar figures are provided by OECD (2022): in 2019, on average, 1.2 percent of total government spending was devoted to cultural services, with differences across countries. Subnational governments accounted for almost 60 percent of total public expenditure towards cultural services and spent on cultural services, on average, 3 percent of their total expenditure. Overall, the above data show that cultural services account for a small component of government budgets.

Comparable and reliable official data on the size of government spending for libraries are not easily available.[47] Few scattered data are provided for some countries by specific studies. According to Curcic (2023), in 2020 the US public libraries' overall funding amounted to $14.61 billion, with almost 94 percent coming from the various levels of government (local, state, and federal) and, among them, local funding accounted for the largest share of libraries' incomes (77%) and the federal level for the smallest one (0.63%).[48] A recent comparison of 12 European countries shows a marked variation of spending on public libraries per inhabitants, ranging from 60.1 euros per inhabitant in Finland to 11.2 euros in Germany, with differences among countries also in terms of organization, decision levels and funding models. (Hageberg, 2023).[49]

The allocation of public cultural expenditure follows different institutional arrangements across countries, depending on the role played by central and local governments, arm's length bodies and the 'space' left to the private and non-profit sector (Mignosa, 2016).[50] Moreover, as for the wider cultural field (OECD, 2022), direct public expenditure can take places in different ways. On one side, a vertically integrated model implies the public production of library services through public libraries and/or through the financing of public institutions owning and managing libraries (schools, universities, research centres, territorial bodies, etc.). On the other side, other actors are involved, through the outsourcing of management, or providing subsidies or grants to private and/or non-profit independent producers. Different incentives are at stake, depending on whether and how the performance of libraries is evaluated[51] by the funding body as well as on the rules governing the funding, for instance the type of subsidy that is provided.[52]

However, direct expenditure is not the end of the story. In fact, government support may also imply indirect spending, so-called tax expenditure, that is, the revenue foregone because of tax concessions granted to cultural institutions or to individuals and companies supporting the arts and culture.

Tax concessions for charitable contributions are widespread all over the world[53] with different features.[54] Comparing the United States and Europe, tax concessions for charities are much larger in the former, a plausible explanation being the importance of public support in European countries and the related lower private support (O'Hagan, 2020). Also, the property tax exemption for non-profit organizations is applied in both, while the reduced value added tax (VAT) on cultural goods and services is important in Europe (O'Hagan, 2020).[55]

It is worth noting that, being not reported in public budgets, the level of tax expenditures can only be estimated, and having different quantitative and qualitative features across countries, it makes any international comparison difficult: a lower level of direct cultural spending, in fact, does not necessarily mean that the size of government support is lower, since the indirect support through taxes might be higher.

Taxes expenditures raise interesting and widely debated theoretical issues (O'Hagan, 2020; Borowiecki et al., 2023). While indirect expenditures provide incentives to private donations and to sponsorship and patronage by large corporations, they raise the issue of shifting the decision about the size and the beneficiaries from elected policy makers to donors, who are not responsible to taxpayers.[56] On one side, such a shift has the positive effect of enhancing the representation of consumers' preferences through their willingness to donate but, on the other side, these preferences might be in favour of conventional activities rather than in favour of innovative and more risky ones and/or would support well established and well-known cultural institutions rather than the small ones[57] (Towse, 2019). Moreover, when donations are prevalent sources of income for cultural organizations, they are likely to affect the organization's behaviour (Frey & Meier, 2006) because donors can exercise some control over the organization's activities and the management will operate to gain a reputation in order to attract funds. A further issue is that the policy-maker is not able to control the overall amount of indirect spending, since it depends on the value of the gift and on the marginal tax rate of the donor.

Whatever form of public financing is implemented – whether direct or indirect – it is important to stress that libraries are anyway funded from tax revenues and, therefore, being in competition with other public services, it is crucial to value their contribution to society well-being.

2.5.2 *Private Funding*

Alongside public funding, libraries have other sources of revenue, important ones being donations and sponsorship.[58] An interesting question refers to the relationship between public funding and private donations to cultural organizations, that is, whether the former increases or decreases the amount of the latter. Empirical evidence is mixed, being based on studies referring to different countries, periods, cultural sectors – mainly performing arts and museums – and type of government support (Borgonovi, 2006).[59] For US libraries, Ferreira Neto (2018) finds a 'crowding in' effect in all levels of government,[60] the policy implication being that the effects to public libraries of reductions of government budgets would be larger than anticipated by policymakers. In some countries, also national lotteries are an important form of philanthropic support to arts and culture (OECD, 2022).[61]

Philanthropy can take place also through crowdfunding,[62] which is increasingly expanding in the cultural field, an interesting feature being that it is not only a source of funding, in the presence of decreasing public support, but also a means to measure consumers' willingness to pay for a project (Benhamou, 2020). Crowdfunding is widespread in the library field (Cortland, 2019),[63] but the question arises whether crowdfunding a community service, such as the one provided by libraries, might be potentially dangerous (Minton, 2017). In fact, crowdfunding for public libraries implies costs not only in terms of human and financial resources subtracted to basic commitments of a public library, but also for library users who may not benefit from having the crowd deciding the services they get.

2.5.3 *Own Resources*

Other sources of funding refer to own resources, that is, funding received from the services sold by libraries. This source of income does not play for libraries the same role as for other cultural institutions such as museums, where entrance fees,[64] royalties for images of the items in the collection[65] and/or other commercial sources of revenue[66] may account for an important share of total income. Apart from superstar libraries, those with unique historical collections and /or located in outstanding buildings worth visiting, where the above arguments apply, in the great majority of libraries the admission is free (non-residents users may be asked to pay) or a nominal fee may be charged for the library card. This is in line with the above-mentioned public and social nature of library activities. Further sources of income may derive from charging fines for overdue materials and fees for specific services (in-library copying and printing, high-definition images of items of the collection, admission fees for programs or events, space rentals, etc.).[67]

Overall, libraries worldwide face the challenge of the constraints of public budgets. To address such a challenge and make libraries' managements sustainable, the diversification of the sources of income and the enlargement of private support in its various forms are possible strategies, even though their impact on the public nature of libraries services has to be carefully taken into account. At the same time it may be important to consider how legal and administrative frameworks impact on such a challenge. In the heritage field, the 'custodianship' model usually leads to heritage underutilization and limits cultural participation (OECD, 2018), negatively impacting the size of benefits generated by heritage.

Notes

1 WTP can be defined as the monetary value an individual attributes to goods and services and is usually represented by the market price.
2 https://librarymap.ifla.org/
3 Around 80% of the libraries currently open worldwide are school libraries and 14% are public libraries. Further details can be found at https://library map.ifla.org/.
4 On the economic features of library services and the motivations for public funding, see Section 2.3.
5 On the different motivations underlying the demand for libraries services, see Chapter 4.
6 Examples might be offered by the libraries located in old monasteries, castles or similar historical buildings.
7 See Chapter 5
8 Salaün (2013) reports the results of bibliometric studies suggesting that 20% of the documents are able to meet 80% of the requests, while almost the entire collection is needed to meet all requests.
9 In parallel with libraries' collections, such a potential is further enhanced through the availability of the Google scanned copies on the Web.

10 This is a finding of an online survey in libraries with 3,348 English-speaking respondents from different geographical areas. For more details on demand, see Chapter 4.

11 The number of physical collection items borrowed per capita in 2019 (5.63), though lower than in 2013 (7.25), is greater than digital collection use per capita (3.53) (Rizzo, 2022).

12 A large survey carried on for academic libraries shows that though the majority of patrons/customers begin their workflows outside the library, afterwards they use and appreciate significantly library services and resources (Hayes et al., 2021).

13 See Chapter 5

14 For academic libraries, a survey suggests that, independently from the use of the library collection, being in a library implies a sense of connection to knowledge itself (Fister, 2009).

15 On the implications for supply and demand see, respectively, Chapter 3 and Chapter 4.

16 In the United States 23% of adults who attended an artistic, creative, or cultural activity did so at community centres or public libraries (National Endowment for the Arts, 2019).

17 In an historical perspective, Black and Pepper (2012) outline that the evolution of the aims of public libraries is reflected in the changes in the public library architectural design, oriented to combine physical and virtual space.

18 To this end, valuation plays a crucial role (see Section 2.3).

19 Denmark, Germany, Hungary, Norway, Sweden and Switzerland.

20 A very extensive literature deals with cultural tourism (see the reviews by Richards, 2018 and Song et al., 2012). The label 'cultural tourism' is taken somehow for granted, though the expanding notion of the cultural consumption of tourists makes the definition increasingly 'elusive' (Noonan & Rizzo, 2017).

21 For instance, Library Planet (https://libraryplanet.net/) is a crowdsourced travel guide for libraries of the world. Examples are provided by Li & Liu (2019), Modeva (2018), Tosic & Lazarevic (2010).

22 For a shortlist, see Kumar (2018).

23 For instance, in 'literary parks' (Donelli et al., 2019).

24 Other capital spending refers to equipment, maintenance of buildings and so forth.

25 For instance, libraries and the items of their collection; in addition to the consumption experiences for users, may also be inputs of different production processes (audio-visual, publishing, etc.), generating further capital formation.

26 A public good is characterized by being non-rival and non-excludable, meaning respectively that its consumption by a single individual does

not prevent its consumption by others and that its consumption cannot be limited to those who pay a price for it. Externalities (or spillover effects) arise whenever the consumption (production) of a good generates positive or negative effects on others, which are not reflected by the market price. 'Existence', 'option' and 'bequest' values, respectively, refer to the fact that people, even if they do not use heritage, may derive benefits from the very existence of heritage, from maintaining the option of consuming it in the future as well as from protecting it for future generations. These non-use values are not recorded by market transactions because no market exists.

27 Alongside the prevalence of positive effects, cultural heritage may provide also negative effects to some people in societies with high (racial, ethnic) heterogeneity, where conflicts are likely to arise, for instance in relation to the sense of identity or the symbolic value of heritage (Snowball, 2013).

28 See Section 2.4.

29 Zbranca et al. (2022) provide a scoping review of these effects related to culture, including libraries in such wider concept.

30 OCLC (2011) outlines that in the United States, in 2010, the Americans who were economically impacted by the recession used libraries more often and valued library services significantly higher than did those not impacted by recession.

31 On the role played by rural public libraries in small-business economic development, see Mehra et al. (2017).

32 Arts Council England (2014) provides some evidence of the 'chain' of effects produced by libraries and generating economic benefits considering five areas: Children's and young people's education and personal development; Adult education, skills and employability; Health and wellbeing; Community support and cohesion; Digital provision. For United States, Manjarrez et al. (2007) focus on the contribution provided by Early Literacy services, Resources and facilities on jobs and careers; Resources and programs for small enterprises and Catalyst role for physical development.

33 On valuation issues, see Section 2.4.

34 See Section 2.5.

35 In this type of relationship, which is very common in public decision-making processes, the *principal* delegates power to the *agent*, who enjoys an informational advantage. In very simple terms, citizens are the *principal* of politicians who, in turn, are the *principal* of bureaucrats. Incentives have to be designed to induce the *agent* to act according to the *principal's* preferences.

36 Martorana et al. (2019), however, also outline that local governments may be biased in favour of 'superstar' heritage because of their touristic attractiveness with respect to 'minor' heritage.

37 Librarianship, as a 'helping' profession, has been compared to psycho-therapy, aimed at problem solving through diagnosis and prescription (Quinn, 2002).

38 Arguments in favour of equity and freedom of information and against censorship/paternalism support the view that librarians should answer all requests for information. The opposite view is supported by the idea that if the use of information may be harmful for society, librarians have a higher obligation to society at large, overriding professional duty.

39 Economic valuation is an important tool to support public decisions at the macro level, to identify the most efficient among several competing proposals, both when funds have to be allocated to various fields (for instance, education, health, culture) as well as within each field (for instance, which historical building, museum or library deserves funding). To this aim, cost-benefit analysis is a widely used methodology (see Box. 2.1).

40 Library case studies implementing these techniques are surveyed in Chapter 4.

41 Highly positive and widely ranging estimates are provided in the litera-ture, using different methods. According to the meta-analysis by Arns et al. (2013) for US libraries the benefit/cost ratio ranges between $5:1 to $6:1. With a wider geographical perspective, and with some overlap-ping, Kim's (2011) review of 15 valuation studies finds benefit/cost ratio estimates from $0.84:1 to $10.33 and Aabø's (2009) meta-analysis on 38 studies finds a range between 1.1 and 10.0.

42 Cultural value is characterized by a multiple set (aesthetic, spiritual, social, historical, symbolic and authenticity) of attributes (Throsby, 2012).

43 To overcome the narrow boundaries of monetary indicator, in heritage projects multi-criteria analysis is used (by architects, conservators, urban planners, etc.) to provide a qualitative evaluation of the different attributes of a project, taking into account stakeholders opinions. For an application to libraries, see Tessler (2013).

44 For a review of the literature on the relationship between economic and cultural values see Angelini & Castellani (2019).

45 The general government sector comprises central government, state gov-ernment, local government and social security funds.

46 Cultural services are covered by COFOG Group 08.2.

47 For European countries, the Council of Europe (2023) provides tables based on data referring to various years, which are not all the same across countries, making any comparison difficult. More details can be obtained by country profiles www.coe.int/en/web/culture-and-heritage/compendium.

48 Funding for US public libraries has increased by 29.04% since 2010, with the local government share increasing by 12.3% over the last 10 years. For further details, see Curcic (2023).

49 The data have been provided within the NAPLE Forum (National Authorities on Public Libraries in Europe) by the librarians of Croatia, the Czech Republic, Denmark, Estonia, Finland, Ireland, Italy, the Netherlands, Norway, Scotland, Slovenia and Sweden. Nordic countries Denmark, Norway and Sweden have the highest level behind Finland, also a Nordic country.

50 For the different institutional arrangements of European countries, see the Council of Europe (2023).

51 On performance measurement issues, see Chapter 3.

52 For the analysis of the different effects of lump-sum and matching grants, see Towse (2019).

53 77% of 177 countries provide some form of incentive to corporate donors while 66% offer some form of incentive to individual donors, both types of incentives being more widespread in high-income countries than in low-income ones (Quick et al., 2014).

54 For instance, income deductions are implemented in the United States, Germany, the Netherlands and Japan; tax credits in Canada and France; or tax refunds in the UK (Hemels, 2020).

55 European countries do apply different VAT rates on printed books and e-books (Council of Europe, 2023).

56 The effects of tax incentives on private giving should not be taken for granted whenever this behaviour has a pro-social element: intrinsic motivations may be undermined or even crowded out by extrinsic incentives and, at the same time, may be affected by the accountability and transparency of the recipient institution (Rizzo, 2021).

57 Evidence of such a bias in the United States in favour of large budget cultural institutions is provided by Sidford (2011).

58 Individual support to cultural heritage organizations can take place not only through monetary contributions but also with time donation and volunteering (Ateca-Amestoy & Gorostiaga 2021), with some evidence that the latter positively affect subjective wellbeing (Ateca-Amestoy et al., 2021). Further on this form of cultural participation, see Chapter 4.

59 On the one hand, the existence of public support for cultural organizations can be considered by donors as a form of certification of quality, while, on the other hand, if the utility function of donors and recipients are interdependent, since the need of the recipient is reduced by public funding, the marginal utility of donors decreases, too.

60 The results suggest a crowd in effect with an inverted U shape in all levels of government: local government would account for an extra 4–6 cents in donation, state government 20–23 cents and the federal government 73 cents to 1 dollar and 33 cents per dollar spent.

61 On the Heritage Lottery Fund, see Clark, K. & Maeer (2008).

62 For further details on crowdfunding, see Chapter 5.

63 Cortland (2019) analyses 174 library and archive projects on Kickstarter and Indiegogo and finds library and archive crowdfunding campaigns raise more money on average and are more likely to successfully meet their funding goals than typical Kickstarter campaigns.

64 Whether to charge entrance fees for museums is highly debated (Fernandez-Blanco & Prieto-Rodriguez, 2020) and various forms of pricing have been proposed, ranging from price differentiation (based on age, membership, or 'friends', local residency, hours, days of the week) to exit prices (depending on the time spent in the museum) (Frey & Steiner, 2012).

65 On the different models for access and use of museum digital collections and for their profitability see Bertacchini & Morando (2003).

66 Merchandising, catering services, and hiring facilities are increasingly used by museums as well as the loan of items from the collection.

67 On fees and fines in US libraries, see Dixon & Gillis (2017). According to Salaün (2013), documentary services are charged because of internal accounting more than for profit purposes.

References

Aabø, S. (2009). Libraries and return on investment (ROI): A meta-analysis. *New Library World*, 110(7/8), 311–324.

Aabø, S., Audunson, R., & Vårheim, A. (2010). How do public libraries function as meeting places? *Library & Information Science Research*, 32(1), 16–26. https://doi.org/10.1016/j.lisr.2009.07.008

Angelini, F., & Castellani, M. (2019). Cultural and economic value: A critical review. *Journal of Cultural Economics*, 43(2), 173–188. https://doi.org/10.1007/s10824-018-9334-4

Arns, J., Williams, R., & Miller, K. A. (2013). *Assessing the value of public library services: A review of the literature and meta-analysis (META)*, www.libsci.sc.edu/MetaWeb/ValuingPublicLibraries_FinalReport.pdf

Arts Council England (2014). *Evidence review of the economic contribution of libraries*. file:///C:/Users/utente/Downloads/Evidence_review_economic_contribution_libraries_2014%20(4).pdf

Ateca-Amestoy, V., & Gorostiaga, A. (2021). Donating money and time to cultural heritage: Evidence from the European Union. *Journal of Cultural Economics*, 46, 101–133. https://doi.org/10.1007/s10824-021-09409-4

Ateca-Amestoy, V., Villarroya, A., & Wiesand, A. J. (2021). Heritage engagement and subjective well-being in the European Union. *Sustainability*, 13(17). https://doi.org/10.3390/su13179623

Audunson, R., Aabø, S., Blomgren, R., Hobohm, H. C., Jochumsen, H., Khosrowjerdi, M., Rudolf Mumenthaler, R., Schuldt, K., Rasmussen, C. H. Rydbeck, K., Tóth, T., & Vårheim, A. (2019). Public libraries as public sphere institutions: A comparative study of perceptions of the public library's role in six European countries. *Journal of Documentation*, 75(6), 1396–1415. https://doi.org/10.1108/JD-02-2019-0015

Benhamou, F. (2020). The economics of crowdfunding. In Bille, T., Mignosa, A. & Towse, R. (Eds.) *Teaching cultural economics*. Cheltenham: Edward Elgar Publishing, 99–104.

Bennet, S., Demas, S., Freeman, G., Frischer, B., Burr Oliver, K., & Peterson (2005). *Library as place: Rethinking roles, rethinking space*. Washington, DC: Council on Library and Information Resources. www.clir.org/wp-cont ent/uploads/sites/6/pub129.pdf

Bertacchini, E., & Morando, F. (2013). The future of museums in the digital age: New models of access and use of digital collections. *International Journal of Arts Management*, 15(2), 60–72. https://www.jstor.org/stable/24587113

Bille, T. (2020). Economic impact studies. In Bille, T., Mignosa, A. & Towse, R. (Eds.) *Teaching cultural economics*. Cheltenham: Edward Elgar Publishing, 69–77.

Bille, T., & Schulze, G. (2006). Culture in urban and regional development. In Ginsburgh, V. & Throsby, D. (Eds.) *Handbook of the economics of art and culture*, Amsterdam: Elsevier, Vol. 1, 1051–1099.

Black, A., & Pepper, S. (2012). From civic place to digital space: The design of public libraries in Britain from past to present. *Library Trends*, 61(2), 440–470. https://doi.org/10.1353/lib.2012.0042

Blamey, R. K., Bennett, J. W., & Morrison, M. D. (1999). Yea-saying in contingent valuation surveys. *Land Economics*, 126–141. https://doi.org/10.2307/3146997

Borgonovi, F. (2006). Do public grants to American theatres crowd-out private donations? *Public Choice*, 126(3/4), 429–451. www.jstor.org/stable/30026762

Borowiecki, K. J., Gray, C. M., & Heilbrun, J. (2023). *The economics of art and culture*. Cambridge: Cambridge University Press.

Bovero, E. (2009). Cultural tourism and libraries. New learning needs for information professionals. In *World library and information congress: 75th IFLA general conference and council*. Milan. www.ifla.org/past-wlic/2009/192-bovero-en.pdf

Chen, T. Y. (1997). A measurement of the resource utilization efficiency of university libraries. *International Journal of Production Economics*, 53(1), 71–80. https://doi.org/10.1016/S0925-5273(97)00102-3

Chung, H. K. (2008). The contingent valuation method in public libraries. *Journal of Librarianship and Information Science*, 40(2), 71–80. https://doi.org/10.1177/0961000608089343

Clark, C., & Hawkins, L. (2011). Public libraries and literacy: Young people's reading habits and attitudes to public libraries, and an exploration of the relationship between public library use and school attainment. London: *National Literacy Trust*. http://files.eric.ed.gov/fulltext/ED515944.pdf

Clark, K., & Maeer, G. (2008). The cultural value of heritage: Evidence from the Heritage Lottery Fund. *Cultural Trends*, 17(1), 23–56. https://doi.org/10.1080/09548960801920302

Cortland, C. (2019). *Crowd funding in libraries: An analysis of library crowd funding project data*. https://cdr.lib.unc.edu/concern/masters_papers/1n79h863t

Council of Europe (2023). *Compendium of cultural policies and trends in Europe*. www.culturalpolicies.net/

Curcic, D. (2023). *Library funding statistics*, Words Rated. https://wordsrated.com/library-funding-statistics/

Del Barrio-Tellado, M. J., Gómez-Vega, M., Gómez-Zapata, J. D., & Herrero-Prieto, L. C. (2021). Urban public libraries: Performance analysis using dynamic-network-DEA. *Socio-Economic Planning Sciences*, 74, 1–15. https://doi.org/10.1016/j.seps.2020.100928

Dixon, J., & Gillis, S. (2017). Doing fine(s)? Fines & fees. *Library Journal* www.libraryjournal.com/story/doing-fines-fines-fees

Donelli, C. C., Fanelli, S., & Mozzoni, I. (2019). Managing and enhancing the intangible heritage: The experience of "Literary Parks". *European Journal of Cultural Management and Policy*, 9(1), 52–63.

Dos Santos, V. F. (2009). Public Libraries and their contribution towards economic development: A discussion. *LIBRES: Library & Information Science Research Electronic Journal*, 19(2), 1–9. https://doi.org/10.32655/LIBRES.2009.2.3

Eftec (2005). *Valuation of the Historic Environment – the scope for using results of valuation studies in the appraisal and assessment of heritage-related projects and programmes*. Final Report. https://historicengland.org.uk/images-books/publications/valuation-historic-environment/valuation-historic-environment-final-rep/

Elliott, D. S., Holt, G. E., Hayden S. W., & Holt, L. E. (2007). *Measuring your library's value: How to do a cost-benefit analysis for your public library*. Chicago: American Library Association.

Eurostat (2023). *Government expenditure on cultural, broadcasting and publishing services*. https://ec.europa.eu/eurostat/statistics-explained/index.php?title=Culture_statistics_-_government_expenditure_on_cultural,_broadcasting_and_publishing_services&oldid=554580

Fernandez-Blanco, V., & Prieto-Rodriguez, J. (2020). Museums. In Towse, R. & Navarrete Hernández, T. (Eds.) *Handbook of cultural economics*, 3rd ed. Cheltenham: Edward Elgar Publishing, 349–357.

Ferreira Neto, A. B. (2018). Charity and public libraries: Does government funding crowd out donations? *Journal of Cultural Economics*, 42(4), 525–542. https://doi.org/10.1007/s10824-018-9318-4

Fister, B. (2009). The glorious study hall: How libraries nurture a life of the mind. *Library Issues*, 30(2), 1–4. https://homepages.gac.edu/~fister/LibraryIssuesNov09.pdf

Frey, B. S. (2005). *What values should count in the arts? The tension between economic effects and cultural value.* Institute for Empirical Research in Economics University of Zurich, Working Paper n. 253.

Frey, B. (2020). Public support. In Towse, R. & Navarrete Hernández, T. (Eds.) *Handbook of cultural economics*, 3rd ed. Cheltenham: Edward Elgar Publishing, 449–456.

Frey, B. S., & Meier, S. (2006). The Economics of museums. In Ginsburgh, V. & Throsby, D. (Eds.) *Handbook of the economics of art and culture.* Amsterdam: Elsevier, 1017–1047.

Frey, B. S., & Steiner, L. (2012). Pay as you go: A new proposal for museum pricing. *Museum Management and Curatorship*, 27(3), 223–235. https://doi.org/10.1080/09647775.2012.701994

Fujiwara, D. (2013). *A general method for valuing non-market goods using wellbeing data: three-stage wellbeing valuation.* CEP Discussion Paper n. 1233, Centre for Economic Performance.

Fujiwara, D., & Campbell, R. (2011). *Valuation techniques for social cost-benefit analysis: Stated preference, revealed preference and subjective well-being approaches a discussion of the current issues.* https://assets.pub lishing.service.gov.uk/government/uploads/system/uploads/attachment_d ata/file/209107/greenbook_valuationtechniques.pdf

Haab, T. C., Interis, M. G., Petrolia, D. R., & Whitehead, J. C. (2013). From hopeless to curious? Thoughts on Hausman's "dubious to hopeless" critique of contingent valuation. *Applied Economic Perspectives and Policy*, 35(4), 593–612. https://doi.org/10.1093/aepp/ppt029

Hageberg, A. O. (2023). Finland spends six times as much as Germany on public libraries. *Bok & bibliotek*. https://bokogbibliotek.no/nyheter/finland-spends-six-times-as-much-as-germany-on-public-libraries-5491/

Halpin, E., Rankin, C., Chapman, E. L., & Walker, C. (2015). Measuring the value of public libraries in the digital age: What the power people need to know. *Journal of Librarianship and Information Science*, 47(1), 30–42. https://doi.org/10.1177/0961000613497746

Hammond, C. J. (2002). Efficiency in the provision of public services: A data envelopment analysis of UK public library systems. *Applied Economics*, 34(5), 649–657. https://doi.org/10.1080/00036840110053252

Hausman, J. (2012). Contingent valuation: From dubious to hopeless. *Journal of Economic Perspectives*, 26(4), 43–56. DOI: 10.1257/jep.26.4.43

Hayes, M. A., Henry, F. A., & Shaw, R. (2021). *Librarian Futures: Charting librarian patron behaviors and relationships in the networked digital age.* Lean Library. www.leanlibrary.com/wp-content/uploads/Librarian_Future s_Lean_Library_2021-1.pdf

Hemels, S. (2020). Tax incentives for the cultural sector. In Bille, T., Mignosa, A. & Towse, R. (Eds.) *Teaching cultural economics.* Cheltenham: Edward Elgar Publishing, 79–85.

IFLA-UNESCO (2022). *Public library manifesto, 2022.* https://repository. ifla.org/bitstream/123456789/2006/1/IFLA-UNESCO%20Public%20Libr ary%20Manifesto%202022.pdf

Imholz, S., & Arns, J. W. (2007). *Worth their weight: An assessment of the evolving field of library valuation.* New York: Americans for Libraries Council. www.actforlibraries.org/pdf/WorthTheirWeight.pdf

Kells, S. (2019). Friday essay: The library—humanist ideal, social glue and now, tourism hotspot. *The Conversation*, 30. https://theconversation.com/ friday-essay-the-library-humanist-ideal-social-glue-and-now-tourism-hots pot-116432

Kim, G. (2011). A critical review of valuation studies to identify frameworks in library services. *Library & Information Science Research*, 33(2), 112–119. https://doi.org/10.1016/j.lisr.2010.09.006

Kritikos, K. C. (2018). Delisting and ethics in the library: Anticipating the future of librarianship in a world that forgets. *IFLA Journal*, 44(3), 183–194. https://doi.org/10.1177/0340035218773783

Kumar, M. (2018). *25 beautiful libraries around the world you have to see*, August 27. https://travel.earth/beautiful-libraries-around-the-world/

Lawton, R. N., Fujiwara, D., Arber, M., Maguire, H., Malde, J., O'Donovan, P., Lyons, A., & Atkinson, G. (2020). *DCMS rapid evidence assessment: Culture and heritage valuation studies—technical report.* London: Simetrica Jacobs, 110. https://assets.publishing.service.gov.uk/ media/600ae69ed3bf7f05bae222e4/REA_culture_heritage_value_Simetr ica.pdf

Lee, S. J., & Chung, H. K. (2012). Analysing altruistic motivations in public library valuation using contingent valuation method. *Library & Information Science Research*, 34(1), 72–78. https://doi.org/10.1016/j.lisr.2011.05.001

Lee, S. J., Chung, H. K., & Jung, E. J. (2010). Assessing the warm glow effect in contingent valuations for public libraries. *Journal of Librarianship and Information Science*, 42(4), 236–244. https://doi.org/10.1177/096100061 0380819

Leguina, A., Mihelj, S., & Downey, J. (2021). Public libraries as reserves of cultural and digital capital: Addressing inequality through digitaliza-tion. *Library & Information Science Research*, 43(3), 1–9. https://doi.org/ 10.1016/j.lisr.2021.101103

Li, Y., Liu, X. (2019). "Library + Tourism": A new direction for the sustainable development of libraries, paper presented at: IFLA WLIC 2019 - Athens, Greece - Libraries: dialogue for change, 22–23 August 2019, Pythagoreion, Samos, Greece. https://library.ifla.org/id/eprint/2703/1/S09-2019-li-en.pdf

Manjarrez, C. A., Cigna, J., & Bajaj, B. (2007). *Making cities stronger: Public library contributions to local economic development.* Urban Institute. https://webarchive.urban.org/uploadedpdf/1001075_stronger_cities.pdf

Martorana, M. F., Mazza, I, Mignosa, A., & Rizzo, I. (2019). The eco-nomics of heritage: Some implications of devolution. In Kunizaki, M.,

Nakamura, K., Sugahara, K. & Yanagihara, M. (Eds.) *Advance in Local Public Economics. Theoretical and Empirical Studies*. Cham: Springer International publishing, 249–260.

Mazza, I. (2020). Political Economy. In Towse, R. & Navarrete Hernández, T. (Eds.) *Handbook of cultural economics*, 3rd ed. Cheltenham: Edward Elgar Publishing, 430–440.

Mehra, B., Bishop, B. W., & Partee, R. P. (2017). Small business perspectives on the role of rural libraries in economic development. *Library Quarterly. Information, Community, Policy*, 87(1), 17–35.

Mignosa, A. (2016). Theory and practice of cultural heritage policy. In Rizzo I. & Towse, R. (Eds.) *The artful economist*. Cham: Springer, 227–244.

Minton, A. (2017). Civic crowd funding is privatisation masquerading as democracy. *The Guardian*. www.theguardian.com/cities/2017/oct/24/civic-crowdfunding-erodedemocracy-local-authority

Modeva, M. (2018). *Libraries as participants in cultural tourism*. www.resea rchgate.net/publication/328725965_Libraries_as_participants_in_cultu ral_tourism

National Endowment for the Arts (2019). *US patterns of arts participation: A full report from the 2017 survey of public participation in the arts*. Washington. www.arts.gov/impact/research/publications/us-patterns-arts-participation-full-report-2017-survey-public-participation-arts

Noonan D. S., & Rizzo I. (2017). Economics of cultural tourism: Issues and perspectives. *Journal of Cultural Economics*, 41, 95–107. https://doi.org/10.1007/s10824-017-9300-6

O' Hagan, J. (2020). Tax concessions. In Towse, R. & Navarrete Hernández, T. (Eds.) *Handbook of cultural economics*, 3rd ed. Cheltenham: Edward Elgar Publishing, 494–502.

OCLC (2005). *Perceptions of libraries and information resources. A report to the OCLC membership*. OCLC Online Computer Library Center. www. oclc.org/content/dam/oclc/reports/pdfs/Percept_all.pdf

OCLC (2011). *Perceptions of libraries, 2010: Context and community. A report to the OCLC membership*. OCLC Online Computer Library Center. https://files.eric.ed.gov/fulltext/ED532601.pdf

OECD (2018). *The value of culture and the creative industries in local development*. Paris: OECD Publishing. www.oecd.org/cfe/leed/2018-SACCI-Handbook.pdf

OECD (2022). *The culture fix. Creative people, places and industries, Local Economic and Employment Development (LEED)*. Paris: OECD Publishing. https://doi.org/10.1787/991bb520-en

Peacock, A. T. (1994). *A future for the past: The political economy of heritage*. Edinburgh: David Hume Institute.

Peacock, A. T. (1997). Toward a workable heritage policy. In Hutter M. & Rizzo I. (Eds.) *Economic perspectives on cultural heritage*. London: MacMillan, 225–235.

Philbin, M., Parker, C. M., Flaherty, M. G., & Hirsch, J. S. (2019). Public libraries: A community-level resource to advance population health. *Journal of Community Health*, 44, 192–199. https://doi.org/10.1007%2Fs10 900-018-0547-4

Provins, A., Pearce, D., Ozdemiroglu, E., Mourato, S., & Morse-Jones, S. (2008). Valuation of the historic environment: The scope for using economic valuation evidence in the appraisal of heritage-related projects. *Progress in Planning*, 69(4), 131–175. https://doi.org/10.1016/j.progr ess.2008.01.001

Quick, E., Kruse, T. A., & Pickering, A. (2014), *Rules to give by: A global philanthropy legal environment index.* Washington, DC: Nexus/McDermott Will & Emery/Charities Aid Foundation. https://idis.org.br/wp-content/ uploads/2014/12/RULES-TO-GIVE-BY-FINAL-with-Country-Repo rts.pdf

Quinn, B. (2002). How psychotherapists handle difficult clients: Lessons for librarians. *Reference Librarian*, 36(75/76), 181. https://doi.org/10.1300/ J120v36n75_17

Richard, G. (2018). Cultural tourism: A review of recent research and trends. *Journal of Hospitality and Tourism Management*, 36, 12–21. https://doi. org/10.1016/j.jhtm.2018.03.005

Rizzo, I. (2021). Behaviourally informed heritage policies: Challenges and perspectives. In Herrero, L. C. & Prieto-Rodríguez, J. (Eds.) *La economía de la cultura: una disciplina jóven.* Oviedo: Ediciones de la Universidad de Oviedo, 59–76.

Rizzo, I. (2023). Is the past sustainable? An economic perspective. In Militello, P. & Panagiotopoulos, D. (Eds.) *Modelling archaeological landscapes. bridging past and present in two Mediterranean Islands.* Heidelberg: Heidelberg University Press, 141–151.

Rizzo, N. (2022). State of US public libraries–more popular & digital than ever. *Words Rated*, February, 17. https://wordsrated.com/state-of-us-pub lic-libraries/

Salaün, J. M. (2013). The immeasurable economics of libraries. In Rizzo, I. & Mignosa, A. (Eds.) *Handbook on the economics of cultural heritage.* Cheltenham, UK: Edward Elgar Publishing, 290–306.

Seaman B. A. (2020). Economic impact of the arts. In Towse, R. & Hernández, T. N. (Eds.) *Handbook of cultural economics.* Cheltenham, UK: Edward Elgar Publishing, 241–253.

Seymour, T. (2022). What is a museum? Icom finally decides on a new definition. *The Arts Newspaper*, 24 August 2022. www.theartnewspaper.com/ 2022/08/24/what-is-a-museum-icom-finally-decides-on-a-new-definition

Sidford, H. (2011). *Fusing arts, culture and Social change: High impact strategies for philanthropy.* Washington, DC: National Committee for

Responsive Philanthropy. www.ncrp.org/wp-content/uploads/2016/11/Fusing_Arts_Culture_and_Social_Change-1.pdf

Skelly, L., Stilwell, C., & Underwood, P. G. (2015). Correlations between the economy and public library use. *The Bottom Line: Managing Library Finances*, 28(1/2), 26–33. https://doi.org/10.1108/BL-12-2014-0032

Snowball, J. D. (2013). The economic, social and cultural impact of cultural heritage: Methods and examples. In Rizzo, I. & Mignosa, A. (Eds.) *Handbook on the economics of cultural heritage*. Cheltenham: Edward Elgar Publishing, 438–455.

Song, H., Dwyer, L., & Zheng Cao, G. L. (2012). Tourism economics research: A review and assessment. *Annals of Tourism Research*, 39(3), 1653–1682. https://doi.org/10.1016/j.annals.2012.05.023

Stover, M. (2004). The reference librarian as non-expert: A postmodern approach to expertise. *The Reference Librarian*, 42(87–88), 273–300. https://doi.org/10.1300/J120v42n87_10

Subaveerapandiyan, A. (2023). Application of Artificial Intelligence (AI) In libraries and its impact on library operations review. *Library Philosophy and Practice*, (e-journal). 7828. https://digitalcommons.unl.edu/libphilprac/7828 1-19.

Tessler, A. (2013). *Economic valuation of the British Library*. Oxford Economics. https://cercles.diba.cat/documentsdigitals/pdf/E130253.pdf

Throsby, D. (2003). Determining the value of cultural goods: How much (or how little) does contingent valuation tell us? *Journal of Cultural Economics*, 27(3/4), 275–85. https://doi.org/10.1023/A:1026353905772

Throsby, D. (2012) Heritage economics: A conceptual framework. In Licciardi, G. & Amirtahmesebi, R. (Eds.) *The economics of uniqueness. Investing in historic city cores and cultural heritage assets for sustainable development*. Washington: The World Bank, 45–74.

Tosic, V., & Lazarevic, S. (2010). The role of libraries in the development of cultural tourism with special emphasis to the Bibliotheca Alexandria in Egypt. *UTMS Journal of Economics*, 1(2), 107–114.

Towse, R. (2019). *A textbook of cultural economics*. Cambridge: Cambridge University Press.

Vårheim, A. (2014). Trust in libraries and trust in most people: Social capital creation in the public library. *The Library Quarterly*, 84(3), 258–277. https://doi.org/10.1086/676487

Vårheim, A. (2017). Public libraries, community resilience, and social capital. *Information Research*, 22(1), 1–19. https://munin.uit.no/bitstream/handle/10037/12470/article.pdf?sequence=2&isAllowed=y]):1-19

Vårheim, A., Steinmo, S., & Ide, E. (2008). Do libraries matter? Public libraries and the creation of social capital. *Journal of Documentation*, 64(6), 877–892. https://doi.org/10.1108/00220410810912433

Weckert, J., & Ferguson, S. (1993) Ethics, reference librarians and expert systems, *Australian Library Journal*, 42(3), 172–181. https://doi.org/10.1080/00049670.1993.10755642

Wright, W. C., & Eppink, F.V. (2016). Drivers of heritage value: A meta-analysis of monetary valuation studies of cultural heritage. *Ecological Economics*, 130, 277–284. https://doi.org/10.1016/j.ecolecon.2016.08.001

Zbranca, R., Dâmaso, M., Blaga, O., Kiss, K., Dascl, M. D., Yakobson, D. & Pop, O. (2022). *CultureForHealth Report. Culture's contribution to health and well-being. A report on evidence and policy recommendations for Europe*. CultureForHealth. Culture Action Europe. www.cultureforhealth.eu/news/the-cultureforhealth-report-is-now-available/

3 The Supply of Library Services

3.1 Introduction

Libraries are multiproduct entities. As we discussed in Chapter 2, they supply some economically and socially valuable services: the conservation, as well as the access to (physical and electronic) collections – books and, marginally, other items including tapes, video, drawings, records, antique manuscripts, maps, and so forth, and some ancillary services, such as workshops, courses, readings, and so forth – which are becoming increasingly important.[1] In providing the above services (and fulfilling the respective functions) libraries have strong analogies with other cultural institutions, namely museums and, especially, public archives. The latter shares with libraries a specific and relevant feature: namely, that provided services are generally free of charge, with a few exceptions.[2] As has been pointed out in the previous chapter, such a feature makes the economic evaluation of libraries more challenging than for other economic entities. Nonetheless, several contributions in the economic literature as well as in other strands of literature have assessed the economic analysis of (some specific types of) libraries, using different methods to evaluate the organizational performance of libraries. Such interest in analyzing the economics of libraries traces back to the late 1960s, with the seminal papers of Newhouse & Alexander (1972), and Goddard (1973).[3] In this chapter we analyze the economics of libraries from the supply-side perspective. More specifically, in Section 3.2 we study the pseudo production function of libraries, reviewing the most relevant issues regarding the provision of library services, as resulting from the economic literature on the efficiency and performance of libraries. An overview of the stages of production is provided in Sections 3.3.

DOI: 10.4324/9781003331896-3

Finally, we account for organizational and external factors (Section 3.4) affecting public library provision.

3.2 The Economic Analysis of Libraries Provision

3.2.1 The Pseudo-production Function of Libraries

Like any other economic entity producing commodities or providing services, public libraries activities can be economically represented as (pseudo-) production processes involving the use of input(s) to produce output(s). Its characterization is, however, not straightforward, for many reasons. First, because of the non-profit nature of the majority of libraries, the identification and the measurement of inputs and outputs are often challenging. Second, the production function varies with the types of libraries, reflecting their different purposes (see on this point Chapter 2). Third, the type of library affects its internal organization, the degree of autonomy in the use and acquisition of inputs, as well as the category of users. Finally, the existence of networks of libraries brings up the problem of coordination among them. Nonetheless, the library pseudo-production function presents some features that are independent of their specific type.

A basic snapshot of libraries' pseudo-production process should at least consider that libraries provide access to their collections, often referred to as book circulation, by using inputs such as a collection of items, which include mainly, but not necessarily only, books, the employed staff and facilities (space, shelves, seating, etc.). As has been pointed out in Chapter 2, a more realistic and comprehensive view of libraries' activities would involve two stages at least. The first one entails the activity of collecting items, their preservation (Guccio et al., 2018), whose weight is lower than for other cultural institutions (such as museums and archives)[4] and organization (including cataloguing), the final one being provision of the loan service to registered users and the access to visitors, as well as the provision of ancillary services. Such a more realistic view of library's functioning implies the analysis of each single stage, which in turn involves studying the different sets of inputs and (intermediate) outputs at play. It also brings up the problem of internal coordination of different stages and the choice of the optimal allocation of resources among them, potentially resulting in a trade-off arising from running the multiple stages (Guccio et al., 2018; 2020; De Witte & Geys, 2011).

From a different and more commonly adopted perspective, the characterization of the production process as being two-stage can be justified also on the grounds of a key feature of several public services provision, which is known in the economic and public administration literature as users' (or consumers') co-production (Whitaker, 1980). In fact, with respect to the provision of services such as education, health care, police, utilities and so forth, 'without the productive activities of consumers nothing of value will result' (Parks et al., 1981, 1002). More specifically, from the concept of co-production it follows that public service provision implies a two-stage process, where the first stage involves the production of a *service potential*, which, in turn, is transformed in the observed outputs in the second stage (De Witte & Geys, 2011). Therefore, such last-stage outputs are partially or totally beyond the control of the provider (Hammond, 2002; De Witte & Geys, 2013), and thus are not really 'produced' by them (De Witte & Geys, 2011). As for libraries, book circulation – that is, the last stage output – strictly depends on users demanding books for loan and, thus, is not as much under the control of librarians as, for instance, the amount of accessible items or the opening hours. Such a distinction must be taken with caution as, for instance, libraries may affect observed outputs such as book circulation through providing some ancillary services, such as courses, lectures, readings, and so forth to facilitate and actively promote reading (De Witte & Geys, 2011).

However, library provision can be studied and evaluated from several different perspectives, and indeed the economic literature on this topic reflects the manifold nature of library provision. In what follows we will take into account that the characterization of library service provision, as a two-stage process, involves the joint consideration of supply- and demand-side aspects. Though, the core of this chapter is the analysis of the supply of library service, that is, how public libraries combine inputs to provide outputs that are under their direct control, which implies studying their efficiency.

3.2.2 The Measurement of Public Libraries' Efficiency

Efficiency and, more in general, performance can be studied using different methods. The use of performance indicators has been very widespread, especially in the past, due to their computation easiness (Worthington, 1999).[5] Performance indicators are ratios of either a single output (or even outcome) on a single input (and are often referred to as productivity indicators), or indicators of the actual or potential demand to proxy scale of operations. Nevertheless, its computational easiness does not come at no cost. In fact, in the context of a multi-input/multi-output service provision, their usefulness is relatively limited (Worthington, 1999), as they do not allow for a comprehensive evaluation of efficiency. For these reasons, studies on the library provision in recent times have increasingly used frontier-estimation technique (either parametric such as the Stochastic Frontier Analysis - SFA -, or non-parametric, such as the Data Envelopment Analysis – DEA and the Free Disposal Hull – FDH) that allow for handling more complex production or provision processes and robustly controlling for exogenous factors affecting efficiency (see Box 3.1. for a snapshot of such techniques).

Box 3.1 Frontier Estimation Techniques

Frontier estimation techniques are nowadays widely adopted in academic works on public sector efficiency assessments. Such techniques are based on the seminal works by Koopmans (1951) and Debreu (1951), empirically applied by Farrell (1957). The frontier approach involves comparison of the actual performance of each observed unit with the optimal performance of those located on the estimated frontier (which is often referred to as the best practice frontier) and returns a measure of the relative (in)efficiency of each single unit with respect to the best performers.

Two main classes of techniques have been developed to estimate efficiency frontiers: namely, parametric and non-parametric frontier models. The most known parametric estimator is the Stochastic Frontier Analysis (SFA – Aigner et al., 1977; Meeusen & Van den Broeck, 1977). Its main disadvantage relies on the need for an a priori identification of the functional for the production process, which is not required by the much more flexible non-parametric alternatives. Among these, the Free Disposal Hull (FDH) and Data Envelopment Analysis (DEA – Charnes et al., 1978) estimators have been increasingly used in public performance evaluation, despite some limitations and some measurement issues, partially overcome by several recent developments. A critical issue for both approaches relies on the identification, selection, and measurement of the relevant set of inputs and outputs, on which bases the frontier has to be estimated and the relative efficiency measured. In many cases such variables are either not directly observable or not easy to quantify in monetary terms. Different types of variables can be handled, including quantitative (not necessarily monetary) and qualitative variables.

A remarkable advantage of frontier techniques over others, such as indicators, is that they allow for assessing the influence of environmental and contextual factors, that is, those variables that are external to the production process, and thus out of the control of providers, but (potentially) affect it. This is particularly important in those countries that are characterized by relevant structural socio-economic gaps among areas. In such contexts, differences in efficiency levels partially depend on differences in the operational environment. Two consequences arise from the above issue. First, relative efficiency measured without controlling for the environmental factors is generally flawed. Second, if the operational environment matters, the economic analysis of service provision should take into account such aspect, and policies designed to improve providers' efficiency should hit it as much as they hit internal features.

From the empirical point of view, analyzing the economics of a library's provision requires the identification of the relevant inputs and outputs as well as of the production function: that is the way different combinations of inputs translate into output levels. The characterization of the functional form of the library provision process is, however, similar to other public services provision. Although a few studies use parametric techniques (e.g., Vitaliano, 1997; Hemmeter, 2006), the abovementioned DEA and FDH (and their recent developments) have been increasingly adopted in the last decade to deal with the issue of studying library provision.

In what follows, we run our economic analysis following library provision stage to stage, thus implicitly assuming that libraries' services cannot be studied comprehensively using a single-stage approach. We choose to model library provision as a two-stage process, thus following the most recent works on this field (Guccio et al., 2018; Del Barrio et al., 2021). In so doing, we assume that libraries use basic inputs to provide a *service potential*. This *service potential* is in fact an intermediate output that is used as an input, jointly with those of the first stage, to co-produce in the second stage the observable outputs of libraries, and, among them the main one, namely the circulation of books. The above characterization of library provision entails a specific identification of the relevant inputs, intermediate outputs and final outputs – identification that is not however unanimously accepted. Hence, we discuss alternative characterizations, thus trying to reflect the different views on this topic. Starting with the first stage we cover the main inputs and then the outputs, that is the *service potential*. Inputs of the first and second stage generally overlap. Staff, facilities, collection (where it is not considered as an intermediate output) are very often used in the empirical literature and although their role in the stage presents few peculiarities, inputs will be discussed only in the analysis of the first stage.

Conversely to inputs selection, no consensus exists in the literature with respect to outputs (Van House, 1984). This is partially due to the modeling of the production process of libraries – that is, whether considering a single or more stages and whether controllable or co-produced outputs are considered – but also depends on the type and function of the evaluated libraries. However, it has been noted (Vitaliano, 1997) that output measurement is structurally imperfect for service provision evaluation, especially because measuring the quality of provision is generally challenging. In fact, quality of provision relies also on often omitted aspects such as the timing of processing requests or the courteousness of the staff (Vitaliano, 1997). Final (second stage) outputs partially differ depending on the type of library. Thus, we separate general to specific ones, where the latter regards outputs that are relevant only for single categories of libraries.

3.3 A Multi-stage Analysis

3.3.1 *The First Stage: Collection, Conservation, and* Service Potential *Provision*

In the very first stage, public libraries collect items that are catalogued and conserved and are used as an input of the provision of the *service potential*. Such activities are undertaken using (capital and labour) inputs, including facilities, staff, financial resources. As is common in the cultural field, the production process is labour intensive and is characterized by high investment, and variable costs. Thus, the sector suffers from the Baumol's cost disease (Baumol & Bowen, 1965; 1966), that is, the increase in the unitary cost of labour due to stagnant productivity combined with the increase in the wages (driven by the fast growing productivity sectors[6]).

Libraries' collections generally consist of a wide range of items, such as books, journals, tapes, maps, and other documents. The number of items owned is often used in the efficiency literature as a proxy for capital stock, given the scarce availability of alternative measures (Worthington, 1999). Though, the collection represents an input of the service provision but is, in turn, the output of collection and conserva-tion activities-requiring specific professional figures-entailing for loan pieces the often-neglected distinction between owned and available. In fact, the total collection is the result of a process of accumulation (and depletion) that is carried on among periods, making collection a quasi-fixed input in the short run (Del Barrio et al., 2021). With few exceptions (e.g. Shim & Kantor, 1999), studies do not disentangle the different types of items collected, thereby implicitly assuming that no differences exist in the way libraries use them for their provision. In turn, this assumption entails the idea that preservation is not a particu-larly relevant activity for libraries. A further distinction is between physical and electronic items, which brings up the related problem of the use and diffusion of digital technologies in library provision (see Chapter 5).

A second relevant input of this and the following stages is the employed staff, generally including skilled and unskilled, profes-sional and support, voluntary, and paid employees. The large majority of studies do not make differences among the above types and use the total number of workers. Among the few studies disentangling staff into categories, Shim & Kantor (1999) consider professional, support staff, and student employees. However, differences exist from the theoretical point of view from several perspectives. First, skilled and unskilled workers generally serve different purposes and some tasks, such as item preservation, or digital services provision, require workers with specific qualifications. Second, being a paid or a voluntary worker may affect productivity and more in general the incentive to maximize the effort. According to IFLA LMW, voluntary staff is particularly relevant for community libraries, accounting for

80 percent of the total staff (on average, 1.6 volunteers per library), thus reflecting the purpose and role of such type of libraries. However, they are quite relevant for public libraries as well (40% of the staff). Such remarkably high shares can be possibly explained with the recent trends in Western countries that have harshened budget constraints for the public sector and for local governments, especially (Halpin et al., 2015). Volunteers are relevant, though to a lower extent, for academic ones (19%), while they represent less than 10 percent of the staff for national (which however have, on average about 10 volunteers each) and are almost absent in school libraries. Thus, full time employees represent more than the 90 percent for national school and other libraries, and 60 percent for public libraries reflecting the need for trained staff for such libraries.[7]

From a more comprehensive perspective, libraries employ librarians (that is workers with specific professional training and skill regarding the library work), archivists, curators, Information and Communication Technology (ICT) specialists and so forth. Since the 1970s, librarians, as well as curators and archivists have experienced relevant difficulties in finding jobs (Roderer, 1983). As soon as ICT began to be increasingly adopted by public libraries as well as other cultural institutions, such as museums (Guccio et al., 2022; Cavalieri et al., 2023) and public archives (Guccio et al., 2021),[8] ICT specialists have grown in importance with respect to more traditional professional positions. Though, two phenomena have slowed down the process of restructuring the staff according to the needs, challenges and opportunities due to innovations and, in general, changes in cultural industries and markets, thus reducing the potential effects of new technologies (Guccio et al., 2021). Namely, legal restrictions exist regarding the recruitment and, especially, the dismissal of workers in the public sector, and public budget constraints limit the turnover, especially in the EU (Nicholas et al., 2010). The presence of different professional positions in public libraries brings up the problem of internal coordination and organization. This aspect is clearly beyond the scope of this study, and generally external to the economic literature, however it must be mentioned that the existence of internal organizational dysfunctions for libraries (as well as for other institutions) has been acknowledged as a relevant issue potentially threatening libraries economic self-sustainability and, in turn, their survival (Acadia, 2020). Notwithstanding, overstaffing or inappropriate combinations of different professional positions, jointly with a rigid demarcation of tasks, have been recognized sources of low efficiency (Vitaliano, 1997).

The very large majority of libraries are located in a single building, often shared with other offices (as in the case of school and academic libraries). Shelves, seating positions, available surface area, but also, depending on the type of library, the size of the institution owning the library as well as related proxies (such as the number of students for school or university libraries (Bernardo et al., 2020 survey) are generally used in the literature as inputs. Facilities are often over-allocated (Vitaliano, 1997), and may even be considered at least partially as a non-discretionary input, given that they are often provided by the financing institution. Of course, library endowment includes furniture, photocopiers, laptops, equipment and so forth. but data on this is generally missing.

The appropriate characterization of public libraries' provision process should consider the provision of the discretionary output, that is, the *service potential*, which includes the already discussed available collection, as well as the opening hours, the seating capacity, including the provision of digital equipment, the ancillary services, (Kantor, 1984), collection addition and number of serial subscriptions, as well as other services such as training courses, activities for children, programs for exhibiting artwork, and offering of space to local community for any use (Fujiwara et al., 2019; Del Barrio et al., 2021).[9]

3.3.2 The Second Stage: Producing Final Outputs

The service potential, jointly with the inputs used in the first stage, is then transformed into final outputs. Book circulation, that is often proxied by the number of loans, has been recognized as the major general final output of library service provision since the early studies (Van House, 1984) and remains the most widely used output,[10] even in recent ones. Other common outputs are the number of visits, the number of consultations, and the number of registrations (Holy, 2022). Although often included as outputs of the first stage, some variables are sometimes used as final outputs as a proxy for unobservable outcomes. This is the case of the number of additions that is often used to proxy for quality of provision, based on the idea that book additions indicate how up-to-date is the collection (Vitaliano, 1997). The same logic applies to opening hours to the extent to which it measures access, which is an important aspect of quality (Vitaliano,

1997). Also, the number of registered users has been also considered as a carry-over (quasi-) fixed input of such a stage, instead of as an output, based on the idea that the larger the number of registered users, the greater the capacity of a library to attract visitors and loan items (Del Barrio et al., 2021).

As said, the final stage is co-produced by users and results in additional social outcomes whose measurement is generally troublesome. However, in some cases, a subset of the related outcomes of library provision can be measured to some extent. This is the case of academic and school libraries.[11] Such libraries have in fact a different purpose than other libraries, which is not the circulation of books *per se* to the general public, if not to a minor extent, but support to the core activity of the institutions they are part of. Thus, for such types of libraries, students' achievements are often used as output/outcome indicators. Additionally, researchers' and professors' scientific research output are widely used for academic libraries (Kim et al., 2020).

3.4 Other Relevant Aspects of Libraries Provision

3.4.1 *Organizational Issues*

Different types of libraries have different outputs, reflecting the specific target of their provision (i.e., the type of users) but also different functions, which may entail peculiar organizational issues. For instance, the weight and relevance of conservation/preservation is generally higher for national libraries than for school or local ones (Guccio et al., 2018), because of the types of collected items, but also due to legal arrangements.[12] In such cases, providers face restrictions to their discretionary power, resulting in priorities that may negatively affect other functions, such as access (Guccio et al., 2018). Equally, urban libraries provide ancillary activities (such as courses, activity for youngsters, provision of their spaces to external activities) that are not generally provided by other types and are switching them towards cultural centers (Del Barrio et al., 2021).

Library provision may significantly differ not only among types of libraries, but also with respect to their internal organization. So far, few economic studies have been published that explicitly target such an issue. As has been outlined in the previous chapter, a relevant aspect is the type of financing (and managing) institution, (whether a local, a national, or different authority) to the extent to which it may lead to different organizational and structural features, affecting efficiency (Hammond, 2009; Kim et al., 2020), and connected to different motivations (Vitaliano, 1997) and level of political pressure (De Witte & Geys, 2013).

Also, it must be noted that a relevant share of libraries is included in networks, which implies a more complex management and organization of a library's activity within each network as well as an additional service (that is, an additional output), namely interlibrary loan. Networks allow libraries to serve a large and potentially heterogeneous area (Hammond, 2002), and to have a broader and larger *service potential*. The problem of managing library networks has been investigated by Bernardo et al. (2020), who focus on a single academic library system, identifying the strategies to improve the provision within the system.

An additional aspect is the operational scale. Several studies have dealt with this issue. Among them, Worthington (1999) finds that scale effects account for a relevant share of inefficiency, estimates the efficient scale at population level for public libraries in a range of twenty to thirty thousand persons.

3.4.2 *Operational Environment*

Evaluating the efficiency in the provision of any service should not disregard that it strictly depends on the environment in which providers operate. Taking into account differences in the operational environment is key for relative efficiency evaluation, that is to offer a correct picture of differences among providers' efficiency (Daraio and Simar, 2005; De Witte and Kortelainen, 2013). In other words, the operational environment reflects the exogenous factors that affect service provision, being beyond providers' control. In fact, such factors have been often included in the input set as non-discretionary inputs (Worthington, 1999), while more recent developments in frontier techniques allow appropriate control for them as conditioning factors that affect efficiency (Daraio and Simar, 2005).

Environmental factors may be categorized as follows: demand-side, institutional, and other factors. Among demand-side factors, differences in the catchment areas are generally recognized as relevant, that is, population size and density, (Vitaliano, 1998; Hammond 2002; 2009; Holy, 2022), which enlarge the potential demand (De Witte and Geys, 2013) but may simultaneously generate congestion

Table 3.1 Inputs, Outputs, Methods and Sample of Selected Works on Libraries' Efficiency

Authors	Case study	Method	Inputs	Intermediate outputs	Final outputs/outcomes
Vitaliano (1997)	235 public libraries in New York	SFA – cost function	Total variable costs, Collection		Book circulation, Per-week opening hours, Book additions in the year.
Chen (1997)	23 university libraries in Taipei	DEA	Staff, Collection, Acquisition expenditure, Library area, Seating capacity		Attendance, Book circulation, Reference transaction, Reader satisfaction, Service hours, Inter-library loans
Vitaliano (1998)	184 libraries in New York	DEA	**Service potential**: Opening hours; Collection; Number of subscriptions and acquisitions, Book additions		Yearly number of items lent, Number of enquiries processed, Number of requests for specific items processed
Sharma et al. (1999)	47 public Libraries in Hawaii	DEA	Operating total expenditures, Staff, Collection, Opening days		Book circulation, Consultations

Shim & Kantor (1999)	99 academic libraries in the US	DEA	Collection, Net additions during the period, Monographs purchased, Total number of current serial copies, Number of full time, professional staff, Number of full time, support staff, Number of full time equivalents of hourly student employees [Non-discretionary] Total full-time student enrolment, Total full-time graduate student enrolment, Total full-time instructional faculty	Interlibrary lending transactions, Interlibrary borrowing transactions, Number of people who participated in group presentations or instructions, Reference transactions, Book circulation
Worthington (1999)	168 New South Wales local government libraries	DEA with non-discretionary inputs	Gross library expenditure, [Non-discretionary: population, area, aged population, student population, non-residential borrowers, socioeconomic index]	Library issues

(Continued)

Table 3.1 (Continued)

Authors	Case study	Method	Inputs	Intermediate outputs	Final outputs/ outcomes
Hammond (2002)	99 UK public Libraries	DEA	**Service potential**: Opening hours; Collection; Number of subscriptions and acquisitions, Book additions		yearly number of items lent, Number of enquiries processed, Number of requests for specific items processed
Holy (2022)	4660 public municipal libraries in Czech Republic	Chebyshev distance DEA	Total expenditures, Staff, Book collection		Registrations, book circulation, Event attendance, Book additions
Saunders (2003)	112 academic libraries in US and Canada	DEA and SFA – cost function	Total library cost (SFA) Normalized costs (DEA)		Book circulation, Reference questions, Interlibrary loans, Interlibrary borrows, Number of bibliographic instruction sessions, Weekly opening hours
Reichmann (2004), Reichmann et al. (2010)	1) 118 University Libraries in English-Speaking and German-Speaking Countries; 2) 68 University libraries in US, Austria, and Germany	DEA	Staff, Collection		Book circulation, Opening Hours, Collection Additions, Subscriptions

Study	Sample	Method	Inputs		Outputs
Chen et al. (2005)	23 public Libraries in Tokyo		Staff, Collection, Area Population		Registered users, Book circulation
Hammond (2009)	UK public library system	Cost distance function	Staff.		Book circulation, Audio-visual circulation, Number of user requests handled, Enquires processed.
Miidla & Kikas (2009)	20 Estonian public libraries	DEA	Yearly acquisition expenditures, Yearly salary expenditures, Collection, Area		Number of users, Book circulation
Simon et al. (2011)	Libraries in Spain	Malmquist index network DEA	Staff, Area, Expenditures,	Collection, Serial subscriptions, Number of seats, Opening hours multiplied by Number of branches.	Book circulation, interlibrary transactions, documents downloaded.
De Witte & Geys (2011); (2013)	German public libraries; Flemish public libraries	Conditional FDH	Staff, operating expenditure, infrastructure	available books and media, opening hours	
de Carvalho et al. (2012)	37 libraries affiliated to a university in Brazil	DEA	Staff, area, number of volumes		Consultations, loans, Enrollments, User traffic
Shahwan & Kaba (2013)	11 academic Libraries in the Arab States	DEA	Total Expenditures, Staff, Collection		Registered users, Book circulation, Collection additions
Stroobants & Bouckaert (2014)	13 public Libraries in Belgium,	DEA and FDH	Total Expenditures, Operating Expenditures, Staff		Book circulation, Opening hours

(Continued)

Table 3.1 (Continued)

Authors	Case study	Method	Inputs	Intermediate outputs	Final outputs/ outcomes
Srakar et al. (2017)	58 public libraries in Slovenia	DEA	Total Revenues, Staff, Area, Ratio of Service Points to Potential Users		Registered users, Visits, Book circulation, Number of events, Events attendance, Equipment
Guccio et al. (2018)	44 Italian public state libraries	Centralised network DEA	Staff, Expenditure excluding labour costs, Total shelves' dimension in linear meters, Number of seats available.	Collection, Financial value of the assets	Visits and attendance, Consultation of different types of items, Users' requests and enquiries processed, Inter-library loan transactions
Kim et al. (2020)	847 public libraries in Korea	DEA	Staff, Expenditures for all resource materials, Area, Collection, Opening hours, Number of periodicals		Books borrowed, Visitors, Number of people who have made request to the library for its information service
Del Barrio et al. (2021)	24 urban libraries in Medellin (Colombia)		Area, Staff, Computer equipment, [Quasi fixed input: Collection]	Open days, number of activities [Quasi fixed output: Users]	Beneficiaries

Source: Table created by authors.

(De Witte and Geys, 2011). Population is also used to indicate the scale of the library, while area proxies the expenditures needed to provide additional branches (Worthington, 1999; Vitaliano, 1997; 1998). Socio-economic characteristics of the demand may affect the actual demand, such as educational level (Del Barrio et al., 2021), the demographic structure (Worthington, 1999; De Witte & Geys, 2011), the share of students and elderly people (Worthington, 1999; Del Barrio et al., 2021) and the perception of safety in moving in the area (Del Barrio et al., 2021). Other factors may include the distance from (county/regional) capitals (Holy, 2022) reflecting potential spillovers in education and cultural capital accumulation.[13]

Institutional and political factors may affect the political pressure from citizens and groups towards library provision (De Witte & Geys, 2013). Among them, it is worth mentioning: the ideological stance of local government, which has been found relevant for municipal public libraries, and the source of public funding, either local of regional, following the idea that voters' interest in public provision efficiency is higher, the more directly they pay for it. Other institutional elements may more directly affect efficiency, such as the wage of directors that Vitaliano (1998) finds to be negatively associated with efficiency.

Overall, the extensive empirical literature on libraries' efficiency provides interesting insights into the main issues related to the provision of library services. These insights, though not conclusive, may represent a useful support for public decision-making, which is especially relevant for public services that are provided for free are not subject to any market valuation.

Notes

1 See above Chapter 2.
2 Generally, libraries are open to registered customers. Registration is very often free, while some ancillary services, such as printing, are usually charged. For more details, see above, Chapter 2.
3 See Van House (1984) for a survey of the very first generation of economic studies on this topic.
4 This is not true for historical libraries, however (Salaün, 2013). As for public libraries in general, in the Enumerate Core survey 4 -2017, only the 85% of libraries declared to have collections to be preserved for

future generations. The shares is close to 100% for museums and galleries (Europeana, 2017). However digital technologies are increasing the relative relevance of preservation for public libraries (Copeland & Barreau, 2011), as discussed in Chapter 5.

5 Worthington (1999) uses performance indicators to evaluate library provision, although jointly with DEA. Specifically, this study uses the gross library expenditure per capita and the library issues per capita.

6 The diffusion of digital technologies partially affected these features. See Chapter 5.

7 Our elaboration on data drawn from the LMW.

8 For an overview of the extent to which digital technologies have been employed by cultural institutions as a whole in the EU, see Guccio et al. (2016).

9 Though, depending on provision characterization, the above variables have been in some cases considered as (non-discretionary) inputs. For instance, opening hours has been included in a single case (Saunders, 2003) among the inputs as a proxy for facility usage to estimate efficiency of academic libraries, where students use facilities to study without borrowing books.

10 According to Holy (2022), more than the 93% of studies use book circulation as output.

11 See Tavares et al. (2018) and Bernardo et al. (2020) for a comprehensive meta-analysis on efficiency studies targeting academic libraries.

12 Many countries require any publisher to deposit any published material to a recognized national institution, commonly a national library. In the last decade, such obligation has been extended to digital materials as well in several countries (Larivière, 2001).

13 For more details on demand, see Chapter 4.

References

Acadia, S. (2020). The organizational trap-gap framework: A conceptual view of library dysfunction. *Ifla Journal*, 46(1), 72–87. https://doi.org/10.1177/0340035219870199

Aigner, D. J., Lovell, C. A. K., & Schmidt, P. (1977). Formulation and estimation of stochastic frontier production functions. *Journal of Economics*, 6, 21–37. https://doi.org/10.1016/0304-4076(77)90052-5

Baumol, W. J., & Bowen, W. G. (1965). On the performing arts: The anatomy of their economic problems. *The American Economic Review*, 55(1/2), 495–502. www.jstor.org/stable/1816292

Baumol, W. J., & Bowen, W. G. (1966). *Performing arts. The economic dilemma. A study of problems common to theater, opera, music and dance.* New York: The Twentieth Century Fund.

Bernardo, M., de Souza, M. A. M., Lopes, R. S. M., & Rodrigues, L. F. (2020, in press). University library performance management: Applying zero-sum gains DEA models to resource allocation. *Socio-Economic Planning Sciences*, 1–9. https://doi.org/10.1016/j.seps.2020.100808

Cavalieri, M, Ferrante, L, Martorana, M. F., & Rizzo, I. (2023). The ICT strategy of Italian museums: Institutional, supply and demand side drivers. *Economics of Innovation and New Technology*, 1–21. https://doi.org/10.1080/10438599.2023.2222268

Charnes, A., Cooper, W. W., & Rhodes, E. (1978). Measuring the efficiency of decision making units. *European Journal of Operational Research*, 2, 429–444. https://doi.org/10.1016/0377-2217(78)90138-8

Chen, T. Y. (1997). A measurement of the resource utilization efficiency of university libraries. *International Journal of Production Economics*, 53(1), 71–80. https://doi.org/10.1016/S0925-5273(97)00102-3

Chen, Y., Morita, H., & Zhu, J. (2005). Context-dependent DEA with an application to Tokyo public libraries. *International Journal of Information Technology & Decision Making*, 4(3), 385–394. https://doi.org/10.1142/S0219622005001635

Copeland, A. J., & Barreau, D. (2011). Helping people to manage and share their digital information: A role for public libraries. *Library Trends*, 59(4), 637–649. DOI: 10.1353/lib.2011.0016

Daraio, C., & Simar, L. (2005). Introducing environmental variables in non-parametric frontier models: A probabilistic approach. *Journal of Productivity Analysis*, 24, 93–121. https://doi.org/10.1007/s11123-005-3042-8

Debreu, G. (1951). The coefficient of resource utilization. *Econometrica: Journal of the Econometric Society*, 19(3), 273–292. https://doi.org/10.2307/1906814

De Carvalho, F. A., José Jorge, M., Filgueiras Jorge, M., Russo, M., & Oliveira de Sá, N. (2012). Library performance management in Rio de Janeiro, Brazil: Applying DEA to a sample of university libraries in 2006–2007. *Library Management*, 33(4/5), 297–306. DOI 10.1108/01435121211242335

Del Barrio-Tellado, M. J., Gómez-Vega, M., Gómez-Zapata, J. D., & Herrero-Prieto, L. C. (2021). Urban public libraries: Performance analysis using dynamic-network-DEA. *Socio-Economic Planning Sciences*, 74, https://doi.org/10.1016/j.seps.2020.100928.

De Witte, K., & Geys, B. (2011). Evaluating efficient public good provision: Theory and evidence from a generalised conditional efficiency model for public libraries. *Journal of Urban Economics*, 69(3), 319–327. https://doi.org/10.1016/j.jue.2010.12.002

De Witte, K., & Geys, B. (2013). Citizen coproduction and efficient public good provision: Theory and evidence from local public libraries. *European*

Journal of Operational Research, 224(3), 592–602. https://doi.org/10.1016/j.ejor.2012.09.002

De Witte, K., & Kortelainen, M. (2013). What explains performance of students in a heterogeneous environment? Conditional efficiency estimation with continuous and discrete environmental variables. *Applied Economics*, 45(17), 2401–2412. https://doi.org/10.1080/00036846.2012.665602

Europeana (2017). *D.4.4 Report on ENUMERATE core survey 4*. Available at the url: https://pro.europeana.eu/files/Europeana_Professional/Proje cts/Project_list/ENUMERATE/deliverables/DSI-2_Deliverable%20 D4.4_Europeana_Report%20on%20ENUMERATE%20Core%20Sur vey%204.pdf

Farrell, M. J. (1957). The measurement of productive efficiency. *Journal of the Royal Statistical Society: Series A (General)*, 120(3), 253–281. https://doi.org/10.2307/2343100

Fujiwara, D., Lawton, R. N., & Mourato, S. (2019). More than a good book: contingent valuation of public library services in England. *Journal of Cultural Economics*, 43, 639–666. https://doi.org/10.1007/s10824-019-09369-w

Goddard, H. C. (1973). Analysis of social production functions-public library. *Public Finance Quarterly*, 1(2), 191–204.

Guccio, C., Martorana, M., Mazza, I., Pignataro, G., & Rizzo, I. (2020). An assessment of the performance of Italian public historical archives: Preservation vs utilisation. *Journal of Policy Modeling*, 42(6), 1270–1286. https://doi.org/10.1016/j.jpolmod.2019.12.006

Guccio, C., Martorana, M. F., Mazza, I., Pignataro, G., & Rizzo, I. (2022). Is innovation in ICT valuable for the efficiency of Italian museums? *European Planning Studies*, 30(9), 1695–1716. https://doi.org/10.1080/09654313.2020.1865277

Guccio, C., Martorana, M. F., Mazza, I., & Rizzo, I. (2016). Technology and public access to cultural heritage: The Italian experience on IT for public historical archives. In Borowiecki, K.J., Forbes, N. & Fresa, A. (Eds.) *Cultural Heritage in a changing world*, Heidelberg: Springer, 55–76.

Guccio, C., Martorana, M. F., Mazza, I., & Rizzo, I. (2021). Back to the Future. Does the use of information and communication technology enhance the performance of public historical archives? *Journal of Cultural Economics*, 45(1), 13–43. https://doi.org/10.1007/s10824-020-09385-1

Guccio, C., Mignosa, A., & Rizzo, I. (2018). Are public state libraries efficient? An empirical assessment using network Data Envelopment Analysis. *Socio-Economic Planning Sciences*, 64, 78–91. https://doi.org/10.1016/j.seps.2018.01.001

Halpin, E., Rankin, C., Chapman, E. L., & Walker, C. (2015). Measuring the value of public libraries in the digital age: What the power people need to know. *Journal of Librarianship and Information Science*, 47(1), 30–42. https://doi.org/10.1177/0961000613497746

Hammond, C. J. (2002). Efficiency in the provision of public services: A data envelopment analysis of UK public library systems. *Applied Economics*, 34(5), 649–657. https://doi.org/10.1080/00036840110053252

Hammond, C. J. (2009). The effect of organisational change on UK public library efficiency. *International Journal of Production Economics*, 121(1), 286–295. https://doi.org/10.1016/j.ijpe.2009.04.027

Hemmeter, J. A. (2006). Estimating public library efficiency using stochastic frontiers. *Public Finance Review*, 34(3), 328–348. https://doi.org/10.1177/1091142105284844

Holý, V. (2022). The impact of operating environment on efficiency of public libraries. *Central European Journal of Operations Research*, 30(1), 395–414. https://doi.org/10.1007/s10100-020-00696-4

Kantor, P. B. (1984). *Objective performance measures for academic and research libraries*. Washington, DC: Association of Research Libraries.

Kim, C., Kim, H., & Choi, K. (2020). Efficiency analysis of public library services based on establishing entity and outsourcing. *Sustainability*, 12(21), https://doi.org/10.3390/su12219205.

Koopmans, T. (1951). An analysis of production as an efficient combination of activities. In Koopmans, T.C. (Ed.) *Activity analysis of production and allocation, Cowles Commission for Research in Economics*, Monograph 13. New York: Wiley, 33–37.

Larivière, J. (2001). *Guidelines for legal deposit legislation*. UNESCO. https://unesdoc.unesco.org/ark:/48223/pf0000121413

Meeusen, W., & van den Broeck, J. (1977). Efficiency estimation from Cobb–Douglas production function with composed error. *International Economic Review*, 18(4), 435–444. https://doi.org/10.2307/2525757

Miidla, P., & Kikas, K. (2009). The efficiency of Estonian central public libraries. *Performance Measurement and Metrics*, 10(1), 49–58. https://doi.org/10.1108/14678040910949684

Newhouse, J. P., & Alexander, A. J. (1972). *An economic analysis of public library services*. Washington, DC: Rand Corporation.

Nicholas, D., Rowlands, I., Jubb, M., & Jamali, H. R. (2010). The impact of the economic downturn on libraries: With special reference to university libraries. *Journal of Academic Librarianship*, 36(5), 376–382. https://doi.org/10.1016/j.acalib.2010.06.001

Parks, R. B., Baker, P. C., Kiser, L., Oakerson, R., Ostrom, E., Ostrom, V., Percy, S.L., Vandivort, M.B., Whitaker, G.P., & Wilson, R. (1981). Consumers as coproducers of public services: Some economic and institutional considerations. *Policy Studies Journal*, 9(7), 1001–1011. https://doi.org/10.1111/j.1541-0072.1981.tb01208.x

Reichmann, G. (2004). Measuring university library efficiency using data envelopment analysis. *Libri*, 54(2), 136–146. https://doi.org/10.1515/LIBR.2004.136

Reichmann, G., & Sommersguter-Reichmann, M. (2010). Efficiency measures and productivity indexes in the context of university library benchmarking. *Applied Economic*, 42(3), 311–323. https://doi.org/10.1080/0003684070 1604511

Roderer, N. K. (1983). *Library human resources: A study of supply and demand*. Washington, DC: National Center for Education Statistics (ED).

Salaün, J. M. (2013). The immeasurable economics of libraries. In Rizzo, I. & Mignosa, A. (Eds.) *Handbook on the economics of cultural heritage*, Cheltenham, UK: Edward Elgar Publishing, 290–306.

Saunders, E. S. (2003). Cost Efficiency in ARL academic libraries, *The Bottom Line: Managing Library Finances*, 16(1), 5–14. https://doi.org/ 10.1108/08880450310464009

Shahwan, M. T., & Kaba, A. (2013). Efficiency analysis of GCC academic libraries: An application of data envelopment analysis. *Performance Measurement and Metrics*, 14(3), 197–210. https://doi.org/10.1108/ PMM-07-2013-0023

Sharma, K. R., Leung, P., & Zane, L. (1999). Performance measurement of Hawaii state public libraries: An application of Data Envelopment Analysis (DEA). *Agricultural and Resource Economics Review*, 28(2), 190–198. doi: 10.1017/S1068280500008182

Shim, W., & Kantor, P. B. (1999). Evaluation of digital libraries: A DEA approach. In *Proceedings of the Annual Meeting-American Society for Information Science*, 36, 605–615.

Simon, J., Simon, C., & Arias, A. (2011). Changes in productivity of Spanish university libraries. *Omega*, 39(5), 578–588. https://doi.org/10.1016/ j.omega.2010.12.003

Srakar, A., Kodrič-Dačić, E., Koman, K., & Kavaš, D. (2017). Efficiency of Slovenian public general libraries: A data envelopment analysis approach. *Lex localis–Journal of Local Self-Government*, 15(3), 559–581. https://doi. org/10.4335/15.3.559-581(2017)

Stroobants, J., & Bouckaert, G. (2014). Benchmarking local public libraries using non-parametric frontier methods: A case study of Flanders. *Library & Information Science Research*, 36(3–4), 211–224. https://doi.org/10.1016/ j.lisr.2014.06.002

Tavares, R. S., Drumond, G. M., Angulo Meza, L., & Mexas, M. P. (2018). Efficiency assessment in university libraries. *Transinformação*, 30, 65–79. https://doi.org/10.1590/2318-08892018 000100006

Van House, N. A. (1984). Research on the economics of libraries. *Library Trends*, 32(4), 407–23.

Vitaliano, D. F. (1997). X-inefficiency in the public sector: The case of libraries. *Public Finance Review*, 25(6), 629–643. https://doi.org/10.1177/ 109114219702500604

Vitaliano, D. F. (1998). Assessing public library efficiency using data envelopment analysis. *Annals of Public and Cooperative Economics*, 69(1), 107–122. https://doi.org/10.1111/1467-8292.00075

Whitaker, G. P. (1980). Coproduction: Citizen participation in service delivery. *Public Administration Review*, 40(3), 240–246. https://doi.org/10.2307/975377

Worthington, A. (1999). Performance indicators and efficiency measurement in public libraries. *Australian Economic Review*, 32(1), 31–42. https://doi.org/10.1111/1467-8462.00091

4 The Demand for Library Services

4.1 Introduction

The consumption of cultural goods and services is extensively examined in the cultural economics literature from different perspectives (Towse, 2019). The theory of demand aims at explaining consumers' choices, taking into account economic factors, such as price and income, focusing attention mainly on museums, performing arts and cultural industries products (such as cinema, books, music, etc.) while disregarding the demand for libraries and archives services; the complementary studies of participation look at other variables, such as age, family background, education, and so forth, and the related surveys usually also include library visits. Studies on cultural demand and participation are also very useful for marketing strategies of for-profit and non-profit suppliers (Towse, 2019). As McKenzie & Shin (2020, p. 216) outline, 'a one-size-fits-all approach to studying demand for cultural products makes no sense' since cultural products are very heterogeneous and exhibit different economic features. Thus, in what follows, some hints deriving from the research on cultural heritage demand, because of its analogies with libraries, will be briefly reviewed.

Some cultural goods and services are provided through non-market systems either free of charge – for instance those supplied by public libraries, archives or some heritage sites and museums – or charging a price without covering the cost of production, such as is the case for most public cultural institutions. Distributional issues as well as policy implications arise when production costs are funded by government and, therefore, borne by taxpayers (Towse & Navarrete Hernández, 2020).

DOI: 10.4324/9781003331896-4

Investigating demand and participation determinants may provide useful hints to policy-makers to improve the effectiveness of policies aimed at increasing citizens' participation in cultural activities and reducing barriers to access. Moreover, from a management perspective, audience segmentation and the related pricing strategies require the understanding of price elasticity as well as information on demand patterns.

The main drivers of market and non-market demand as well as consumers' motivations are investigated in Section 2, while Section 3 presents data on cultural participation in a comparative perspective.

4.2 In Theory ...

4.2.1 Cultural Goods as 'Experience Goods'

The demand for cultural goods might be considered just like the demand for ordinary goods in the sense that it responds to prices (own and related) and income. Cultural goods, however, cannot be fully assimilated to normal goods because of some peculiar features that require special consideration (McKenzie & Shin, 2020).

They have symbolic elements, and individuals need adequate skills to appreciate and enjoy their consumption (Ateca-Amestoy, 2013). In fact, as it is widely stressed, unlike normal goods, cultural goods are 'experience goods', such a term being used in cultural economics with different meanings, referring to the fact that individuals' appreciation increases with experience or that cultural goods can be evaluated by individuals only when they get information through their consumption, or that experience is an end in itself, this last meaning being used in marketing economics (Towse, 2019). As reported by Hutter (2011) the notion of experience applies with some difference to various industrial branches in the cultural field, with libraries being identified as 'experience areas', with experience as a primary goal and no relevant role for creativity.

The individual's ability needed to judge the quality of cultural goods depends on the level of human capital, as determined by formal education and earlier cultural experiences, the latter being considered also as a form of individual cultural capital.[1]

Traditionally, a distinction is drawn between *highbrow* culture (for instance, fine arts or classical concerts) and *lowbrow* culture (such as visiting fairs), the former requiring cultural capital and education, with the latter being less intellectually demanding and more aimed to entertainment. Such a distinction tends to lessen, with *highbrow* consumers being increasingly omnivorous (de Vries & Reeves, 2022).[2] However, the relative importance of education is found to vary across cultural activities, with a higher impact on more intellectually demanding forms of culture (Suarez et al., 2020).

The relationship between cultural experiences and past behaviour to explain cultural consumption has been widely investigated by cultural economists, the most quoted models being the 'rational addiction' model and the 'learning-by-consuming' model. The former (Stigler & Becker, 1977) is based on the idea that each consumption experience (namely of music) enhances its appreciation, and results in more consumption capital, that is knowledge about it, which reduces the time cost of future consumption, while tastes do not change. In the latter (Levy-Garboua & Montmarquette, 1996), individuals learn how to appreciate cultural goods and develop tastes as they consume them, which affects future consumption decisions. Thus, both models predict that current cultural consumption depends on past behaviour, though within different processes of taste formation.

4.2.2 Price and Income as Determinants of Demand

As far as price and income are concerned, on the basis of standard models of demand, many studies provide estimates on price and income elasticity mainly with respect to performing arts (Baldin, 2020), cinema (Fernandez-Blanco et al., 2013) and museums (Fernandez-Blanco & Prieto-Rodriguez, 2020), libraries usually being publicly funded without charging a price.[3] Most papers find low-price elasticity, while the income elasticity is usually high and sometimes greater than 1, in line with the assumption that cultural goods might be considered 'luxury' goods (Cameron, 2019). However, results are not clear-cut (for performing arts, Seaman, 2006), and caution is needed because of identification problems[4] and the lack of suitable data on prices (Lévy-Garboua & Montmarquette, 2011). A relevant policy implication of low price elasticity refers to the effectiveness of subsidy policies, since if a cultural good is price inelastic a decrease in its price, induced by government policy, does not have the desired effect in terms of increasing demand.

As for the effects of the price of complementary and substitute goods, also in the access to a cultural good case, it is reasonable to assume that the higher the price of a complementary good, for instance transportation, and the lower the price of a substitute, for instance e-books, the lower the demand for book loans (Ateca-Amestoy, 2013).

In addition to income, time can be a further constraint to individual capacity to consume, varying with respect to the different types of access to cultural heritage, whether 'real' or 'virtual'[5]. The opportunity cost of time is higher for individuals with higher income and/or with less discretionary time, depending on labour market commitments and household responsibilities.[6] Thus, because of their higher opportunity cost of time, higher-income individuals might reduce their consumption of cultural activities in favour of less time-intensive goods, the consequence being that observed income elasticity of demand would be positive but lower than expected.

4.2.3 Non-market Demand

In addition to market demand, it is important also to take into consideration non-market demand, mainly referring to the above-mentioned non-use values. Several studies worldwide have elicited the benefits associated to heritage, including libraries, measuring in monetary terms the Willingness to Pay (WTP) for the non-use values as well as the direct-use values and employing different techniques (Snowball, 2013).[7] Traditionally, this research within cultural economics has extensively investigated mainly built heritage, museums and archaeological sites (Noonan, 2002 and 2003; Eftec, 2005; Wright and Eppink, 2016)[8] and, more recently, a report by Lawton et al. (2020) offers evidence of Contingent Valuation (CV) and Subjective Well Being (SWB) studies in libraries,[9] casting doubts on the reliability of some WTP estimates[10]. In parallel, other strands of literature, namely the Library Information Science and the Library management refer on the increasing application of a variety of non-market techniques on libraries (Imholz & Arns, 2007; Arns et al., 2013; 2023). Recently, the effects of the pandemic on WTP for libraries services have been analyzed with contrasting results. While Gomez-Zapata et al. (2023) find a positive impact on the value of the direct and passive use of libraries, according to Stejskal et al. (2023) the perceived value of book borrowing services did not change during the pandemic period.

Without any claim to being exhaustive, Table 4.1 summarizes the main findings of selected evaluation studies on non-market demand for libraries, representative of different geographical areas, and types of libraries and techniques employed. The differences in quality (Lawton et al., 2020), techniques,[11] scope of the analyses (whether an individual library, a specific service within a library, or a group of libraries), type of library, institutional features (national, local, network) as well as the economic context (emerging economies versus developed countries and large cities or small ones) do not allow for generalizations. Overall, however, the empirical findings confirm that a positive monetary value is assigned to library services,[12] that WTP is lower than WTA, and that values are higher for users than for non-users (see Table 4.1).

4.2.4 Demand Motivations

The demand for heritage responds to different individual motivations, ranging from entertainment to education or scientific ones (Ateca-Amestoy, 2013). The motivations vary very much depending on the specific heritage and on the type of audiences. For instance, when considering libraries all the above holds, with the scientific one being probably more marked than for most other types of heritage.[13] It is worth noting that recreational motivation, usually linked to leisure time, has some peculiar features in the case of the library. In fact, it involves both visitors to historical or specialized libraries attracted by the cultural and historical value of the collections of ancient books and manuscripts or rare and specific items, and users of libraries aimed at borrowing books for reading. It is reasonable to assume that while in the latter case the members of the local community are the main audience, in the former case, the visitors of cultural attractions[14] are mainly cultural tourists. This demand feature has important implications for the strategies of libraries in deciding the composition of their output and for the evaluation of their economic and social effects.

Unlike the more general demand for heritage goods and services, economic motivations may also underlie the demand for library services. As stated above (Chapter 2), evidence from US libraries shows that borrowing books or electronic items has been an alternative to buying them by those in economic difficulties as consequence of the recession (OCLC, 2011).

Moreover, further motivations are likely to be related to the wide array of additional services provided by libraries to the general public as well as to targeted groups of users. In fact, users may find in libraries heterogeneous services such as training courses, terminals

Table 4.1 Selected Estimates of User and Non-user Values

Authors	Case study	Method	WTP /WTA (CV) Value of engagement (SWB)	Sample	Notes
Harless & Allen (1999)	Cabel Library of Virginia Commonwealth University	CV	$5.59. (students' WTP per semester) $45,76 (faculty members' WTP per year) (To maintain the current hours of operation of the reference desk) $2.41 (students' WTP per semester) $9.37 (faculty members' WTP per year) (For additional 18 hours for service desk) $1.37 (students' WTP per semester) $3.46 (faculty members' WTP per year) (For another additional 18.5 hours for service desk)	170 (students) 212 (faculty members)	Estimated B/C of 3.5:1 (current hours of reference desk service) Estimated B/C of 4.9:1 (additional 18 hours for service desk)
Pung et al. (2004)	British Library (London)	CV	£ 273 (reading room users' monthly minimum WTA) £116 (reading room users' monthly WTP) £ 6.30 (UK non-users WTP)	229 (users) 2,030 (UK non-users)	Estimated B/C of 4.4:1

(Continued)

Table 4.1 (Continued)

Authors	Case study	Method	WTP/WTA (CV) Value of engagement (SWB)	Sample	Notes
Aabo (2005)	Norwegian libraries	CV	Within the range of 400 NOK (WTP) and 2,000 NOK (WTA) per household per annum	Overall 999, divided in sub-samples	Estimated B/C ratio of 4:1
Jura Consultants (2005)	15 local libraries in Bolton Metropolitan Borough Council (BMBC)	CV	£ 4.83 (users' average monthly WTA) £ 3.63 (users' average monthly WTP) £ 1.00 (non-users average monthly WTP)	232 (residents of BMBC who used a library in BMBC in the past 12 months) 68 (residents who did not use a library in BMBC in the past 12 months)	Estimated B/C ratio of 1.24:1

Chung (2008)	Jungrang Public Library (Seoul)	CV	500 library visitors (randomly assigned to conventional CV, DM and DM+IBM)	2836 won (median WTP) (conventional CV) 804 won (median WTP) (DM format) 1773 won (median WTP) (DM+IBM format) By type of service (DM+IBM format): 13,083 won (median WTP) (literacy programmes); 339 won (median WTP) (facility use service); 310 won (median WTP) (material use) 128 won (median WTP) (reference service)	Estimated B/C ratio of 2.95:1 (conventional CV). Estimated B/C ratio of 0.84:1 (DM format). Estimated B/C ratio of 1.85:1 (DM+IBM).
Hider (2008)	Wagga Wagga City Library (South Wales, Australia)	CV	300 households, residents in Wagga Wagga or around	$8.27 (mean monthly WTP)	Estimated B/C ratio of 1.33:1

(Continued)

Table 4.1 (Continued)

Authors	Case study	Method	WTP /WTA (CV) Value of engagement (SWB)	Sample	Notes
Baptista Melo & Pacheco Pires (2011)	Portuguese digital library services	CV	€10.5 (professors' average maximum WTP per month) (including null values) €14.9 (professors' average maximum WTP per month) (excluding null values); from €7.8 to €4.9 (different types of students' average maximum WTP per month) (including null values); From €13.7 to €8.6 (different types of students' average maximum WTP per month) (excluding null values)	540 professors 1,240 (PhD, Master and undergraduate students)	Estimated B/C ratio of 1.91:1 (including null values) B/C ratio of 3.32:1 (excluding null values) The valuation is higher for the user groups with higher percentage use of digital services and with higher knowledge of digital services
Ikeuchi et al. (2013)	Japanese libraries	CV	350 JPY (WTP per library-use on average) 374.9 JPY (mean WTP) (type 1 / bigger library) 222.4 JPY (median WTP) (type 1 / bigger library) 340.4 JPY (mean WTP) (type 2 / smaller library) 200.1 JPY (median WTP) (type 2 / smaller library)	1,108 respondents	Household income and frequency of public library use significantly affect WTP

Author (year)	Library	Method	Results	Sample	Findings
Tessler (2013)	British Library (London)	CV	£876 (reading room UK users' monthly WTA); £168 (reading room UK users' monthly WTP); £8.98 (general public all users WTP); £10.99 (general public past users WTP); £8.15 (general public non-users WTP)	2,065 users of reading rooms (both UK and oversea); 1,211 general public (users and non-users)	B/C of 5.1:1 (excluding donations); B/C of 4.9:1 (including donations)
Fujiwara et al. (2014)	British libraries	SWB	£1,359.00 (average per person per year) (monetized increase in wellbeing from using libraries frequently)	6,251 (individuals who go to the library more than once per year)	
Hájek & Stejskal (2015)	Municipal library (Prague)	CV	4,024 CZK (users' minimum WTA) (average); 1,032 CZK (users' WTP per annum) (average) if tax could be reduced by the contribution to the library); 642 CZK (users' WTP per annum) (average)	Overall 2,227	The main determinants of public library value include: income, frequency of the library use and alternative costs (the amount the library saved respondents, e.g. from borrowing books instead of buying them)
Fujiwara et al. (2019)	English local libraries	CV	£19,51 (users' mean WTP per annum); £10.30 (non-users' mean WTP per annum)	Overall around 2,000; 1,250 (users); 735 (non-users)	Respondents using health services, attending lectures and using library space for socializing have on average a higher WTP. Library use is also positively associated with subjective well-being.

(Continued)

Table 4.1 (Continued)

Authors	Case study	Method	WTP /WTA (CV) Value of engagement (SWB)	Sample	Notes
Gomez-Zapata & Del Barrio (2023)	26 public libraries (Medellin, Colombia)	CV	$60,323.51 COP (USD 16.37) (users' mean WTP)	1,731	Estimated B/C of 5.97:1
Gomez-Zapata et al. (2023)	26 public libraries (Medellin, Colombia)	CV	$56,419.79 COP (USD 16.15) (users' mean WTP) $40,261.11 COP (USD 11.53) (non-users' mean WTP) $53,435.84 COP (USD 15.30) (full sample's mean WTP)	1,990 (1,731 users) (259 non-users)	The study was conducted during the pandemic. The significant variables that positively impact WTP are: level of income, user character and level of complementary cultural consumption. The pandemic also positively impacted respondents' WTP statements Motivation for WTP: interest in the cultural good; the possibility of improving education; satisfaction with the services provided; enhanced quality of life; knowledge and altruistic feelings

Source: Table created by authors.

to access the Internet, programs for creating and exhibiting artwork, support for job seeking and, more in general, an area for the local community to use and a meeting place for people with different cultural backgrounds. Thus, motivations of libraries' users appear to be of a wider range than those for other heritage institutions. Villarroya & Ateca-Amestoy (2018), with respect to Spanish libraries, indicate that people's perception of their libraries has changed, with a decline of traditional library services (such as borrowing or reading books) and the arise of new ones (such as learning digital skills, gaining access to digital material or attending scheduled activities). In the United States, while traditional activities, such as borrowing books or reading, are still prevalent, users are also increasingly attending classes and lectures, joining meetings or using computers and the Internet (Horrigan, 2016). Gomez-Zapata & Del Barrio (2023), with respect to public libraries in Medellin, find that the users' highest valuations correspond to libraries' traditional functions (such as loaning out and consulting bibliographical material) followed by services related to educational and leisure activities, while the lowest satisfaction refers to the services related to access to information technology (access to ICT and Internet connection) and loaning out spaces.

Cultural demand is also potentially influenced by other people's choices, the so-called bandwagon effect (Baldin, 2020), peer effects (Albergaria et al., 2020), and word-of-mouth mechanisms,[15] family influences and can also be considered as 'social status signaling' (Seaman, 2020). It is also worth noting that cultural goods are shared goods and, therefore, are likely to reflect common values (Towse, 2019).

4.3 In Practice ...

4.3.1 Types of Cultural Participation

According to UNESCO (2012, p. 51), cultural participation can be defined as 'participation in any activity that, for individuals, represents a way of increasing their own cultural and informational capacity and capital, which helps define their identity, and/or allows for personal expression'.

Three types of cultural participation can be distinguished, depending on how it takes place: attendance, the consumption of cultural content through the media, and active practice (Ateca-Amestoy

& Prieto Rodriguez, 2013). Leaving aside the last one, which is rather outside the scope of this study, it is worth noting that, traditionally, the representation and measurement of cultural participation has focused on the attendance of performing arts and heritage institutions though increasing attention is paid to digitized cultural experiences.[16] The measurement and analysis of cultural participation considers only participation as an expression of conscious and voluntary behaviour. The feature of awareness has become increasingly important in recent years because of the diffusion of forms of 'unintentional' consumption related to the application of technologies (Cicerchia, 2017). Furthermore, volunteering is considered an important dimension of cultural participation (OECD, 2022; Ateca-Amestoy et al., 2021).

A related important phenomenon is non-participation, that is, the fact that some individuals systematically are not engaged in cultural activities, with a distinction between those who are not expected to participate anyway and those who might attend depending on the circumstances – respectively, the so-called 'never goers' and 'potential attenders' (for cinema, Suarez et al., 2022; for performing arts, Montoro-Pons & Cuadrado-García, 2016; for performing arts and museums, Ateca-Amestoy & Prieto Rodriguez, 2013). Distinguishing between different groups of non-attenders may have significant implications for the design of policies aimed at promoting access to cultural activities.[17] Cultural participation is also recognized as a citizen's right with important implications for development (Campagna, 2017).

At a domestic policy level, in most countries promoting access, enlarging the participation in the arts and culture is a widely shared objective because of the several benefits deriving from cultural consumption both for individuals and society. Among the others,[18] it is worth noting that the attendance of cultural activities has, indeed, positive effects on individual well-being, measured as self-reported life satisfaction (Ateca Amestoy et al., 2021) or as happiness and relaxation (Fujiwara & MacKerron, 2015),[19] boosts the cultivation of skills and entrepreneurship (OECD, 2022), favours social interaction contributing to the production of relational goods and social capital (Tavano Blessi et al., 2014), has positive effects on health (Zbranca et al., 2022) and promotes social cohesion and higher participation in civic life (Campagna et al., 2020; Martorana & Mazza, 2023) as well as higher levels of voluntary contributions to the provision of cultural goods (Finocchiaro Castro et al., 2021). Thus, measuring and analyzing cultural participation is important for the design of effective evidence-based cultural policies, to know not only the level and the socioeconomic composition of participation rates, but also the determinants of their variation (O'Hagan, 2017). Moreover, it is worth noting that there may be a complementarity between cultural participation and public expenditure with a bi-directional relationship: on the one hand, publicly financed cultural institutions are able to enlarge their supply and increase attendance and, on the other hand, high levels of cultural participation are likely to favour political consensus for high levels of cultural public spending. (OECD, 2022).[20]

Cultural participation can be studied with different methodological approaches, depending on what are the objectives, the variables of interest and the scope of the analysis (UNESCO, 2012). Being cultural statistics aimed at capturing countries' cultural practices, reflecting their identities, UNESCO (2012) rather than imposing a universal standard, defines core features for the measurement and understanding of cultural participation.[21]

Different sources – official statistics, including surveys, and complementary data sources (e.g., Internet-based data such as TripAdvisor, Google maps, etc.) as well as administrative data – can be used to measure people's engagement in cultural activities. OECD (2022) discusses the main sources of cultural participation data and their limitations. For official data, it is outlined, for instance, lack of continuity across time – since cultural participation is often measured through ad hoc modules within surveys – or coverage at the subnational level. For complementary sources, limitations refer, for instance, to possible underestimation of the level of cultural engagement of specific groups of the population or a downward bias for sites that are more popular in real-life than online.

The availability, the quantity and reliability of administrative data vary across countries as well as within a country in relation to the quality of administrative systems. Following UNESCO (2012), the most common, as far as libraries are concerned, are: number of visits; number of registered library readers; books consulted/lent in libraries; digital visitors to libraries (number of unique logins to the institutions' website).[22]

Surveys are widely used tools at national as well as international levels.[23] To assess the level of engagement in cultural activities, key statistical indicators that are frequently used are participation rate, frequency rate, time spent in cultural participation, and cultural expenditure (UNESCO, 2012). Usually, in most surveys on cultural participation, indicators are analyzed in relation to socio-economic and demographic variables such as age, gender, income, level of education, and professional status.[24]

In what follows, the main results of surveys carried on at European level and in the United States are briefly sketched, with special attention to libraries.[25]

4.3.2 Cultural Participation in Europe

Preliminarily, broadly speaking, it is worth noting that in Europe the type of cultural participation appears to be related to a country's orientation: Southern European countries show higher participation rates in activities with a stronger entertainment component while Northern European countries exhibit high participation in activities with 'high culture' components, such as museum and library attendance, a possible explanation being higher levels of education and public spending (OECD, 2022). Moreover, cultural participation differs not only across European countries but also across regions within each country.

According to the latest available Eurobarometer[26] (European Commission, 2017), participation varies for different cultural activities and ranges widely across activities and countries. Available data refer jointly to libraries and archives, which exhibit the strongest similarities compared with other cultural activities and, for simplicity, from now on, reference in the text will be made only to libraries.

Libraries are less visited than other cultural activities: only 30 percent of respondents have visited a library or archive at least once in a year,[27] while 61 percent have visited a historical monument or site.

The proportions of respondents who have visited a library at least once in the previous 12 months vary widely across the EU, ranging from 51 percent in Denmark and 47 percent in Finland to 10 percent in Greece and 15 percent in Cyprus.

Moreover, unlike other cultural activities, participation in libraries does not appear to be increasing through time. Compared to 2013, in fact, respondents are less likely to have visited a library or archive (-1%)[28] while they are more likely to have visited a museum or gallery (+13%) or a historical monument or site (+9%).

While visits to historical monuments or sites have increased in all countries in the period 2013–2017, library attendance decreased in 20 countries, with the largest decreases in Sweden (-30%) and Finland

(-19%), while visits have increased in 7 countries, with the highest percentages in Luxembourg (+16%) and Austria (+10%).

Library visitors overall exhibit socio-demographic similar characteristics compared to those of cultural heritage sites and museums. Those who are more likely to have visited a library at least once in the previous 12 months are the youngest respondents, aged 15–24 (45%) compared to other age groups; students (54%); respondents with higher numbers of years of education and even more those who are still studying (54%); respondents using the Internet daily (35%); respondents without financial problems (33%); respondents who live close to a form of cultural heritage and those who are somehow personally involved in cultural heritage (33% and 40%, respectively).

As Towse (2019) stresses, closely linked to the use of libraries is the individual consumption of books in their various forms, that is, purchasing books from bookshops (both physically and online), downloading e-books, sharing books in book clubs and reading groups and borrowing them from libraries and friends,[29] Data of a survey of people aged from 20 to 74, carried out from 2008 to 2015 in 15 EU countries[30] (Eurostat, 2018), shows that reading habits are different across countries: the average time spent reading books ranges from 2 minutes a day in France to 13 minutes in Estonia. In Finland, 16.8 percent of the population surveyed recorded reading books as a 'main activity' while, at the opposite end of the scale, France (2.6%) had the lowest share of respondents reading books. In all the surveyed countries, more women read books than men, though the latter read for longer periods than women. As for the link between the use of libraries and reading habits, Bhatt (2010) finds that the use of libraries increases the amount of time an individual spends reading (by approximately 27 minutes on an average day) and the amount of time parents spend reading to/with young children (by 14 minutes).[31]

The reasons for not participating are investigated for all cultural activities without disaggregating data for each specific activity and, therefore, it is not possible to assess whether there are significant differences between the use of libraries and other cultural activities. Overall, the Eurobarometer survey (European Commission, 2017) shows the most important barriers to accessing cultural heritage sites or activities: lack of time (37%), cost (34%), lack of interest (31%) and lack of information (25%). As said before, a further perspective to represent cultural participation is the financial one, which is the measurement of private spending for cultural activities. Eurostat

(2020) data show that nearly 3 percent of EU household consumption expenditure was devoted to cultural goods and services, with a minor share (about 2%) regarding museums, libraries, and zoological gardens, with no specification for each of these cultural institutions. As an indirect reference to libraries, however, it is worth noting that on average 12.3 percent of cultural expenditure was devoted to books.

Finally, looking at cultural engagement at large, the Eurobarometer provides some data on a further dimension, namely private support through donations and/or through volunteering: almost 7 percent of respondents donate money or other resources to an organization that is active in the field of cultural heritage while 5 percent do voluntary work. Also, this dimension of cultural engagement shows marked differences across European countries. In fact, at least one in ten do voluntary work in Sweden (14%), the Netherlands and Ireland (both 11%), Denmark and Slovenia (both 10%), while just 2 percent of respondents in Portugal, Bulgaria, and Lithuania say the same. Respondents in the Netherlands, Malta (both 19%), and Sweden (14%) are the most likely to donate compared to 1 percent of respondents in Greece and 2 percent in Portugal.

Overall, while confirming the importance of income and education as drivers of participation in libraries, the above data show that this activity engages only low percentages of respondents in European countries, though with marked differences across them, suggesting, once again, the importance of institutional context.

4.3.3 *Cultural Participation in the United States*

According to the data provided by the Pew Centre (Horrigan, 2016),[32] 48 percent of Americans visited in person a public library or a bookmobile in 2015, and among them 30 percent visited several times a month or more.

Also in the United States there are differences depending on age, education, gender, race and income. Young adults are more likely to have visited a library (53%) than those aged 65 and older (40%). Americans with college degrees are especially likely to have visited a public library (59%), as are women (57%). Furthermore, 52 percent of blacks and 50 percent of Americans living in households with annual incomes of $30,000 or less have visited the library.

Moving to nonattendance, 19 percent of respondent say they have never visited a public library or a bookmobile: they are more likely to be male (24%), aged 65 and older (26%), Hispanic (32%), Black (28%), high school graduates or less (29%), or living in households earning less than $30,000 (27%).

Data on reading habits in the United States (National Endowment of the Arts, 2019) show that in 2017, 53 percent, of adults had read a book, such a percentage being lower (47%). for the youngest adults (aged 18–24). Of book readers, the highest percentage (51%) reads 1 to 5 books. Women read books at higher rates than men (61% versus 44%) and more educated adults read more than less educated: the percentage of adults with a graduate degree who read (79%) was between 10 and 60 percentage points higher than it was for adults. Considering differences of race/ethnicity, data show that 60 percent of White adults read books compared to Black adults (47%), Hispanic adults (32%) and Asian adults (45%).

Notes

1 However, 'the term "cultural capital" is used in other disciplines to mean something different from its interpretation in economics. In sociology, the term is used, following Pierre Bourdieu, to mean an individual's competence in high status culture. In economic terms, this characteristic of people can be construed as an aspect of their human capital' (Throsby, 2011, p. 146).
2 According to Sacco et al. (2018), this distinction may be considered outdated as a consequence of the changes of cultural production models: the increase of the demand for mass entertainment associated with growth of the cultural and creative industries and, more recently, the increase of the user-generated content, originated by growth of digital platforms, with the consequence of blurring the distinction between consumers and producers.
3 Although, some additional services, such as printing, can be charged.
4 Among other aspects, it is difficult to disentangle income and education effects (Borowiecki et al., 2023).
5 On the effects of technology, see Chapter 5.
6 The combination of the market price and the opportunity cost of time is referred to as the full (shadow) price of the cultural activity (Ateca-Amestoy, 2020).
7 On the relevance of evaluation for the assessment of public libraries, and on the main valuation methods, see Chapter 2.
8 Only three of these studies apply CV to libraries, namely, St. Louis Public Libraries, the reference desk of the Cabel Library of the Virginia Commonwealth University and Norwegian libraries. For details, see Noonan (2002).

9 For a comparative analysis of SWB and CV in museums, see Bakhshi et al. (2015).

10 This report, commissioned by the British Department of Digital Culture Media and Sports (DCMS) carries out a Rapid Evidence Assessment (REA) on 171 values provided by academic papers and grey literature reports, using non-market valuation techniques (such as Revealed Preferences methods, Stated Preferences methods, Well-being Valuation methods and Benefit Transfer) for various types of cultural sites and activities, to identify best practice methods as well as weaknesses.

11 For instance, in CV crucial aspects refer to sample selection, survey design, WTP elicitation format, payment vehicles, modes of survey administration. For a discussion of methodological and implementation issues, see Bakshi et al. (2015).

12 Most studies also calculate positive and very different Benefit/Cost ratios (B/C), which are reported in Box 4.1.

13 In this sense, for archives, see Guccio et al. (2016).

14 For instance, the documentary heritage listed in the Unesco Memory of the World Register. (https://webarchive.unesco.org/20220323041423/https://en.unesco.org/programme/mow/register)

15 On the use of word-of-mouth for libraries' marketing, see Barber & Wallace (2009).

16 See Chapter 5.

17 From a policy perspective, the concepts of access and participation are closely related though different. As the European Commission (2012, p. 7) outlines, the former 'focuses on enabling new audiences to attend cultural activities, removing the barriers to access them, while the latter "recognizes the audience as an active interlocutor, to be consulted – or at least involved – in planning and creating the cultural offer."'

18 The benefits stemming from libraries to society are also examined in Chapter 2.

19 Fujiwara & MacKerron (2015) look at people's self-reported happiness and feelings of relaxation in real time, during the cultural activities using a UK dataset called Mappiness.

20 For selected European countries (Germany, Latvia, Lithuania, Portugal, Spain) a positive correlation between public expenditure on culture and cultural participation is found (OECD, 2022). It is also noted that the increased attendance in publicly supported cultural activities may stimulate private spending in non-publicly financed cultural activities.

21 The 2009 FCS (UNESCO-UIS, 2009) provides a pragmatic definition of culture based on the concept of cultural domains (Cultural and Natural Heritage – including libraries; Performance and Celebration; Visual Arts and Crafts; Books and Press; Audio-visual and Interactive Media; Design and Creative Services; Intangible Cultural Heritage) and related domains

(Tourism; Sports and Recreation), which are identified as the minimum set of core cultural domains for which UNESCO would encourage countries to collect comparative data.

22 Note that such variables are often used in the literature on the evaluation of library efficiency and performance, thus explicitly or implicitly assuming that library outputs are partially co-produced by users. See Chapter 3 for a detailed discussion on this point.

23 An in-depth analysis of the methodological aspects of surveys is outside the scope of this study. For an overview, see UNESCO (2012).

24 Depending on the specific features of the countries, further variables can be taken into consideration, such as, for instance, race/ethnicity, religion, class/caste, language (UNESCO, 2012).

25 More detailed data on cultural participation in libraries are provided by national surveys. For a list of surveys, see UNESCO (2012) and OECD (2022, box 2.7).

26 The Eurobarometer Survey Series was launched by the European Commission in 1974 and monitors the social and political attitudes of the public. Five of these surveys (2001, 2003, 2007, 2013 and 2017) were devoted to cultural participation.

27 16 percent visited a library 1–2 times, 6 percent 3–5 times and 8 percent more than 5 times.

28 The decrease pertains only to those who visited a library more than 5 times (-6%) while those who visited a library 1–2 times increased (+5%).

29 A side effect of the use of libraries is that it can displace the demand of readers for buying books, generating a loss of sales and, therefore, a loss of revenues for authors and publishers. To compensate for these losses, governments have provided the public lending right (PLR) with statutory bodies administering it.

30 The countries surveyed are: Austria, Belgium, Estonia, Finland, France, Germany, Greece, Hungary, Italy, Luxemburg, Malta, Poland, Romania, Spain, and United Kingdom.

31 At the same time, Bhatt (2010) estimates that using libraries reduces the time spent watching television (58 minutes) while there is no significant change in other activities. For children in school, library use positively impacts homework completion rates.

32 The Pew Research Center carried out a telephone survey of 1,601 Americans aged 16 and older from March 7 to April 4, 2016.

References

Aabø, S. (2005). Valuing the benefits of public libraries. *Information Economics and Policy*, 17(2), 175–198. https://doi.org/10.1016/j.infoecopol.2004.05.003

Albergaria, M., & Jabbour, C. J. C. (2020). The role of big data analytics capabilities (BDAC) in understanding the challenges of service information and operations management in the sharing economy: Evidence of peer effects in libraries. *International, Journal of Information Management*, 51, 1–13. https://doi.org/10.1016/j.ijinfomgt.2019.10.008

Arns, J., Williams, R., & Miller, K. A. (2013). *Assessing the value of public library services: A review of the literature and meta-analysis (META)*. www.libsci.sc.edu/MetaWeb/ValuingPublicLibraries_FinalReport.pdf

Arns, J., Williams, R., Miller, K., Von Nessen, J., Cripe, M. A., & Copeland, C. (2023) Furthering Our Understanding of the Economic Value of Public Library Services (META 2). *Institute for museum and library services LG-96-18-0240-18*. https://sc.edu/study/colleges_schools/cic/research/sponsored_awards/meta/meta2/pdfs/meta2_final.pdf

Ateca-Amestoy, V. (2013). Demand for cultural heritage. In Rizzo, I. & Mignosa, A. (Eds.) *Handbook on the economics of cultural heritage*. Cheltenham, UK: Edward Elgar Publishing, 89–110.

Ateca-Amestoy, V. (2020). Participation. In Towse, R. & Navarrete Hernández, T. (Eds.). *Handbook of cultural economics*, 3rd ed., Cheltenham: Edward Elgar Publishing, 399–407.

Ateca-Amestoy, V., & Prieto-Rodríguez, J. (2013). Forecasting accuracy of behavioural models for participation in the arts. *European Journal of Operational Research*, 229, 124–131. https://doi.org/10.1016/j.ejor.2013.02.005

Ateca-Amestoy, V., Villarroya, A., & Wiesand, A. J. (2021). Heritage engagement and subjective well-being in the European Union. *Sustainability*, 13(17), 1–16. https://doi.org/10.3390/su13179623

Baldin, A. (2020). Consumer behaviour in the performing arts. In Bille, T., Mignosa, A. & Towse, R. (Eds.) *Teaching cultural economics*. Cheltenham, UK: Edward Elgar Publishing, 157–166.

Bakhshi, H., Fujiwara, D., Lawton, R., Mourato, S., & Dolan, P. (2015). *Measuring economic value in cultural institutions*. Arts and Humanities Research Council. www.cultureforumnorth.co.uk/wp-content/uploads/2015/11/Measuring-Economic-Value.pdf

Baptista Melo, L., & Pacheco Pires, C. (2011). Measuring the economic value of the electronic scientific information services in Portuguese academic libraries. *Journal of Librarianship and Information Science*, 43(3), 146–156. https://doi.org/10.1177/0961000611411708

Barber, P., & Wallace, L. (2009). The power of word-of-mouth marketing. *American Libraries*, 40(11), 36–39. www.jstor.org/stable/25650454

Bhatt, R. (2010). The impact of public library use on reading, television, and academic outcomes. *Journal of Urban Economics*, 68(2), 148–166. https://doi.org/10.1016/j.jue.2010.03.008

Borowiecki, K. J., Gray, C. M., & Heilbrun, J. (2023). *The Economics of Art and Culture*. Cambridge University Press.

Cameron, S. (2019). Individual choice behaviour. In Cameron, S. (Ed.) *A Research Agenda for Cultural Economics*, Cheltenham, UK and Northampton, MA, USA: Edward Elgar Publishing, 41–62.

Campagna, D. (2017). Implementing the human right to take part in cultural life: Trends and perspectives of inclusive cultural empowerment. *Peace Human Rights Governance*, 1(2), 169–193. 10.14658/PUPJ-PHRG-2017-2-2

Campagna, D., Caperna, G., & Montalto, V. (2020). Does culture make a better citizen? Exploring the relationship between cultural and civic participation in Italy. *Social Indicators Research*, 149(2), 657–686. https://doi.org/10.1007/s11205-020-02265-3

Chung, H. K. (2008). The contingent valuation method in public libraries. *Journal of Librarianship and Information Science*, 40(2), 71–80. https://doi.org/10.1177/0961000608089343

Cicerchia, A. (2017). Measuring participation in the arts in Italy. In Ateca-Amestoy, J., Ginsburgh, V. M., Mazza, V., O'Hagan, I. & Prieto-Rodriguez, J. (Eds.) *Enhancing participation in the arts in the EU challenges and methods.* Heidelberg: Springer, 35–49.

de Vries, R., & Reeves, A. (2022). What does it mean to be a cultural omnivore? Conflicting visions of omnivorousness in empirical research. *Sociological Research Online*, 27(2), 292–312. https://doi.org/10.1177/13607804211006109

Eftec (2005). *Valuation of the Historic Environment – the scope for using results of valuation studies in the appraisal and assessment of heritage-related projects and programmes.* Final Report. https://historicengland.org.uk/images-books/publications/valuation-historic-environment/valuation-historic-environment-final-rep/

European Commission (2012), *Report on policies and good practices in the public arts and in cultural institutions to promote better access to and wider participation in culture*, European Commission DG EAC, Publications Office of the European Union, Brussels. https://ec.europa.eu/assets/eac/culture/policy/strategic-framework/documents/omc-report-access-to-culture_en.pdf

European Commission (2017). *Cultural heritage (Special Eurobarometer 466), Report.* Brussels: European Commission. https://kreatywna-europa.eu/wp-content/uploads/2018/11/EUROBAROMETER_ebs_466_en_final.pdf

Eurostat (2020). *Culture statistics – household expenditure on culture.* https://ec.europa.eu/eurostat/statistics-explained/SEPDF/cache/44962.pdf

Eurostat (2018). *World Book Day.* https://ec.europa.eu/eurostat/web/products-eurostat-news/-/EDN-20180423-1

Fernandez-Blanco, V., Orea, L., & Prieto-Rodriguez, J. (2013). Endogeneity and measurement errors when estimating demand functions with average prices: An example from the movie market. *Empirical Economics*, 4(3), 1477–1496. https://doi.org/10.1007/s00181-012-0587-z

Fernandez-Blanco, V., & Prieto-Rodriguez, J. (2020). Museums. In Towse, R. & Navarrete Hernández, T. (Eds.). *Handbook of cultural economics*, 3rd ed., Cheltenham: Edward Elgar Publishing, 349–357.

Finocchiaro Castro, M., Mazza, I., & Romeo, D. (2021). The role of cultural capital on the voluntary contributions to cultural goods: A differential game approach. *Games*, 12(1), 27. https://doi.org/10.3390/g12010027

Fujiwara, D., Kudrna, L., & Dolan, P. (2014). *Quantifying and valuing the wellbeing impacts of culture and sport*. Department for Culture Media and Sport Research Paper. www.social-value-engine.co.uk/calculator/Quantifying_and_valuing_the_wellbeing_impacts_of_sport_and_cult ure.pdf

Fujiwara, D., Lawton, R. N., & Mourato, S. (2019). More than a good book: Contingent valuation of public library services in England. *Journal of Cultural Economics*, 43, 639–666. https://doi.org/10.1007/s10 824-019-09369-w

Fujiwara, D., & MacKerron, G. (2015). *Cultural activities, art forms and wellbeing*. London, UK: SImetrica, Arts Council England. http://media. wix.com/ugd/9ccf1d_05c61fa6c3ee4ea68de17ce62f71cd53.pdf

Gómez-Zapata, J. D., & del Barrio -Tellado, M. J. (2023). Social impact and return on investment from cultural heritage institutions: An application to public libraries in Colombia. *Journal of Cultural Heritage*, 64, 102–112. https://doi.org/10.1016/j.culher.2023.09.004

Gómez-Zapata, J. D., Herrera-Moreno, M. A., & Herrero-Prieto, L. C. (2023). Valuing cultural public goods in times of pandemic: What happened to the libraries? *Journal of Librarianship and Information Science*, 1–19. OnlineFirst. https://doi.org/10.1177/09610006231196345

Guccio, C., Martorana, M. F., Mazza, I., & Rizzo, I. (2016). Technology and public access to cultural heritage: The Italian experience on IT for public historical archives. In Borowiecki, K. J., Forbe, N. & Fresa, A. (Eds.) *Cultural Heritage in a Changing World*, Heidelberg: Springer, 55–76.

Hájek, P., & Stejskal, J. (2015). Modelling public library value using the contingent valuation method: The case of the Municipal Library of Prague. *Journal of Librarianship and Information Science*, 47(1), 43–55. https://doi.org/10.1177/0961000614525217

Harless, D. W., & Allen, F. R. (1999). Using the contingent valuation method to measure patron benefits of reference desk service in an academic library. *College & Research Libraries*, 60(1), 56–69. https://crl.acrl.org/index.php/crl/article/view/15261/16707

Hider, P. (2008). Using the contingent valuation method for dollar valuations of library services. *The Library Quarterly: Information, Community, Policy*, 78(4), 437–458. https://doi.org/10.1086/591180

Horrigan, J. B. (2016). *Libraries 2016*. Pew Research Center. www.pewresea rch.org/internet/wp-ontent/uploads/sites/9/2016/09/PI_2016.09.09_Librar ies-2016_FINAL.pdf

Hutter, M. (2011). Experience goods. In Towse, R. (Ed.) *Handbook of cultural economics*, 2nd ed., Cheltenham: Edward Elgar Publishing, 211–215.

Ikeuchi, A., Tsuji, K., Yoshikane, F., & Ikeuchi, U. (2013). Double-bounded dichotomous choice CVM for public library services in Japan. *Procedia-Social and Behavioral Sciences*, 73, 205–208. https://doi.org/10.1016/j.sbs pro.2013.02.042

Imholz, S., & Arns, J. W. (2007). *Worth their weight: An assessment of the evolving field of library valuation.* New York: Americans for Libraries Council.. www.actforlibraries.org/pdf/WorthTheirWeight.pdf

Jura Consultants (2005). Bolton's *museum, library and archive services*; An *economic valuation*. https://webarchive.nationalarchives.gov.uk/2012021 5214224/http://research.mla.gov.uk/evidence/documents/bolton_main.pdf

Lawton, R. N., Fujiwara, D., Arber, M., Maguire, H., Malde, J., O'Donovan, P., Lyons, A. & Atkinson, G. (2020). *DCMS rapid evidence assessment: Culture and heritage valuation studies—technical report.* London: Simetrica Jacobs, 110. https://assets.publishing.service.gov.uk/media/600ae69ed3bf7 f05bae222e4/REA_culture_heritage_value_Simetrica.pdf

Lévy-Garboua, L., & Montmarquette, C. (1996). A microeconometric study of theatre demand, *Journal of Cultural Economics*, 20(1), 25–50.

Lévy-Garboua, L. & Montmarquette, C. (2011). Demand. In Towse, R. (Ed.) *Handbook of cultural economics,* 2nd ed., Cheltenham: Edward Elgar Publishing, 177–189.

Martorana, M. F. & Mazza, I., (2023). The effect of social interaction and cultural consumption on voting turnout. In Leroch, M. & Rupp, F. (Eds.) *Power & responsibility: Interdisciplinary perspectives for the 21st century in honor of Manfred J. Holler*. Cham: Springer, 331–343.

McKenzie, J., & Shin, S. Y. (2020). Demand. In Towse, R. & Navarrete Hernández, T. (Eds.) *Handbook of cultural economics,* 3rd ed., Cheltenham: Edward Elgar Publishing, 216–227.

Montoro-Pons, J. D. & Cuadrado-García, M. (2016). Unveiling latent demand in the cultural industries: An application to live music participation. *International Journal of Arts Management*, 18(3), 5–24. www.jstor.org/sta ble/44989661

National Endowment for the Arts (2019). *US Patterns of Arts Participation: a full report from the 2017 survey of public participation in the arts*. Washington. www.arts.gov/impact/research/publications/us-patte rns-arts-participation-full-report-2017-survey-public-participation-arts

Noonan, D. S. (2002). *Contingent valuation studies in the arts and culture: An Annotated bibliography* Cultural policy center at the University of Chicago.

www.researchgate.net/publication/5091244_Contingent_Valuation_
Studies_in_the_Arts_and_Culture_An_Annotated_Bibliography?enric
hId=rgreq-6b69b4144a3b364ae85fedaad0acb26d-XXX&enrichSource=
Y292ZXJQYWdlOzUwOTEyNDQ7QVM6MTAzODA3ODI0NDMz
MTY1QDE0MDE3NjExMjI0ODg%3D&el=1_x_3&_esc=publicationC
overPdf

Noonan, D. S. (2003). Contingent valuation and cultural resources: A meta-
analytic review of the literature. *Journal of Cultural Economics*, 27,
159–176.

O'Hagan, J. (2017). European statistics on participation in the arts and their
international comparability. In Ateca-Amestoy, V.M., Ginsburgh, V.,
Mazza, I., O'Hagan, J. & Prieto-Rodriguez, J. (Eds.) *Enhancing participation in the arts in the EU challenges and methods.* Heidelberg: Springer,
3–18.

OCLC (2011). *Perceptions of libraries, 2010: Context and community.
A report to the OCLC membership.* OCLC Online Computer Library
Center. https://files.eric.ed.gov/fulltext/ED532601.pdf

OECD (2022). *The culture fix. Creative people, Places and Industries.
Local Economic and Employment Development (LEED).* Paris: OECD
Publishing. https://doi.org/10.1787/991bb520-en

Pung, C., Clarke, A., & Patten, L. (2004). Measuring the economic impact
of the British library. *New Review Academic Librarianship*, 10, 79–102.
https://doi.org/10.1080/13614530412331296826

Sacco, P. L., Ferilli, G., & Tavano Blessi, G. (2018). From culture 1.0 to culture 3.0: Three socio-technical regimes of social and economic value creation through culture, and their impact on European Cohesion Policies.
Sustainability, 10(11). https://doi.org/10.3390/su10113923

Seaman, B. A. (2006). Empirical studies of demand for the performing arts.
In Ginsburg V. A. & Throsby, D. (Eds.). *Handbook on the economics of art
and culture*, Vol. 1. Amsterdam: Elsevier, 415–472.

Seaman, B. A. (2020). Demand for cultural goods: Key concepts and a hypothetical case study. In Bille, T., Mignosa, A. & Towse, R. (Eds.) *Teaching
cultural economics.* Cheltenham: Edward Elgar Publishing, 149–156.

Snowball, J. D. (2013). The economic, social and cultural impact of cul-
tural heritage: methods and examples. In Rizzo, I. & Mignosa, A. (Eds.)
Handbook on the economics of cultural heritage, Cheltenham: Edward
Elgar Publishing, 438–455.

Stejskal, J., Zapletal, D., & Prokop, V. (2023). The perceived value of book
borrowing services is stationary in the time of Covid-19: Empirical evidence from the Municipal Library in Prague. *Journal of Librarianship and
Information Science*, 55(4), 948–959. https://doi.org/10.1177/0961000622
1113919

Stigler, G. J., & Becker, G. S. (1977). 'De Gustibus Non Est Disputandum', *American Economic Review*, 67(2), 76–90. www.jstor.org/stable/1807222

Suarez-Fernandez, S., Perez-Villadoniga, M. J., & Prieto-Rodriguez, J. (2020). The changing role of education as we move from popular to highbrow culture, *Journal of Cultural Economics*, 44, 189–212. https://doi.org/10.1007/s10824-019-09355-2

Suarez-Fernandez, S., Perez-Villadoniga, M. J., & Prieto-Rodriguez, J. (2022). Price salience in opinion polls and observed behavior: The case of Spanish cinema. *Economic Modelling*, 111. https://doi.org/10.1016/j.econmod.2022.105848.

Tavano Blessi, G., Grossi, E., Sacco, P. L., Pieretti, G., & Ferilli, G. (2014). Cultural participation, relational goods and individual subjective well-being: Some empirical evidence. *Review of Economics & Finance*, 4(3), 33–46.

Tessler, A. (2013). Economic valuation of the British Library. Oxford Economics. https://cercles.diba.cat/documentsdigitals/pdf/E130253.pdf

Throsby, D. (2011). Cultural capital. In Towse, R. (Ed.) *Handbook of cultural economics*, 2nd ed., Cheltenham: Edward Elgar Publishing, 142–146.

Towse, R. (2019). *A textbook of cultural economics*. Cambridge: Cambridge University Press.

Towse, R., & Navarrete Hernández, T. (2020). Introduction. In Towse, R. & Navarrete Hernández, T. (eds.). *Handbook of cultural economics*, 3rd ed., Cheltenham: Edward Elgar Publishing, 1–8.

UNESCO-UIS (2009). The 2009 UNESCO *framework for cultural statistics*. Montreal: UNESCO Institute of Statistics. https://uis.unesco.org/sites/default/files/documents/unesco-framework-for-cultural-statistics-2009-en_0.pdf

UNESCO (2012). *Measuring cultural participation*. Montreal: UNESCO Institute for Statistics.

Villarroya, A., & Ateca-Amestoy, V. (2018). Changing trends in Spanish library services: Conceptualization and measurement in official statistics. *Journal of Librarianship and Information Science*, 50(2), 216–226. https://doi.org/10.1177/0961000616664400

Wright, W. C., & Eppink, F. V. (2016). Drivers of heritage value: A meta-analysis of monetary valuation studies of cultural heritage. *Ecological Economics*, 130, 277–284. https://doi.org/10.1016/j.ecolecon.2016.08.001

Zbranca, R., Dâmaso, M., Blaga, O., Kiss, K., Dascl, M. D., Yakobson, D., & Pop, O. (2022). *CultureForHealth Report. Culture's contribution to health and well-being. A report on evidence and policy recommendations for Europe*. CultureForHealth. Culture Action Europe. www.cultureforhealth.eu/news/the-cultureforhealth-report-is-now-available/

5   Libraries in a Digital Era

5.1 Introduction

Digital Technologies (DT) have had a massive impact on cultural and creative industries, and on libraries among them, affecting the supply and the demand side, and blurring the distinction between producers and consumers.[1] The application of DT to cultural and creative industries is nowadays very common and widespread, also thanks to public intervention especially in Western countries (Chowdhury, 2014).[2]

More recently, the COVID-19 pandemic has changed the way people interact each other and gain access to goods and services, enhancing the diffusion and development of channels of consumption that have exploited even more the potential of DT.

Clearly, neither the digital revolution nor the Covid-19 pandemic have been the first shocks affecting libraries. In fact, libraries have adjusted to the changes in society throughout their history, continuously evolving, although with marked differences across countries.[3] Their organisation and, even more, their role in society have changed many times (Salaün, 2013). For a long time, libraries have worked as local monopolists in the production, preservation, filtering, and access provision of knowledge. Then, once printing developed as an autonomous industry, libraries have been forced to outsource such functions (Salaün, 2013). Further changes occurred later, especially due to the Industrial Revolution. In more recent times, the role of collectors as gatekeepers and filters of knowledge has been weakened as well, with the dramatic increase of publications and formats, due to the digital revolution. The emerging of Web search engines has further increased the pressure on libraries and changed the traditional borders of libraries' functions. Finally, the DT has induced the emerging of

DOI: 10.4324/9781003331896-5

different business models along the value chain, changing the relative market power of libraries with respect to producers (Cichocki, 2007; Salaün, 2013).[4] As outlined by IFLA (2021),[5] librarians are well aware of the challenges they are facing, and they have searched strategies to reverse threats into opportunities and adapt to the new conditions trying to reassert their role in society. The IFLA has selected five main trends shaping the current and future society that should guide libraries in their development. Perhaps not surprisingly, all of them regard DT.

Adaptation, however, requires organisational flexibility as well as the resources to undertake the needed investments (Noh, 2011; Chowdhury, 2014; Michnik, 2015), including the training of employees (Michnik, 2015). In addition, in some countries cultural and organisational barriers have also limited the extent of such processes (Tammaro, 2020). These features are critical, especially for the public sector, and thus for public libraries for at least two reasons. On the one hand, more binding public budget constraints affect the availability of resources for libraries (Shim, 2003; Shim & Kantor, 1998; Halpin et al., 2015) and limit public investment on ancillary infrastructures (such as network services improvements). On the other hand, legal constraints on the labour market limiting the turnover in the public administration makes it difficult to hire well-trained human resources to tackle technological challenges.

This chapter discusses the above issues and is organized as follows. In the next Section we provide an overview of the changes that have affected cultural institutions in general. Section 3 presents some figures regarding the actual spread of DT among public libraries, compared to that of other cultural institutions. Then, in Section 4, we analyse the theoretical issues related to the effect of DT on the supply of public libraries services with a focus on digital libraries. Finally, Section 5 discusses the effects on the demand.

5.2 The impact of Digital Technologies on Cultural and Creative Industries

5.2.1 Overview of DT Effects

The diffusion of DT has reshaped cultural and creative industries, in turn affecting cultural institutions in several ways. As soon as DT became increasingly accessible, they affected consumption, production and distribution of cultural goods. DT have brought new commodities and new markets with them, opened room to new providers and changed the role of traditional ones. Depending on the specific industry, new private providers have affected the relative market power of traditional ones (Benhamou, 2015), and the average quality of products (Waldfogel, 2020), but have also significantly expanded the access to cultural goods and changed cultural consumption patterns.

Although there is a consensus on their positive effects, DT have showed a flip side as well. From the demand side, DT have opened up room for the spread of a range of behavioral disorders and pathologies (Sacco et al., 2018). Further threats from the supply side include the emerging of new copyright issues (Gasaway, 2010), and the rise of digital piracy (McKenzie, 2020; Waldfogel, 2020), which determined a sale displacement effect, especially on the music and movie sectors.[6] While digital piracy has initially determined a fall in revenues in the music industry especially, it later brought about the development of online platforms in the industries (such as Netflix and Spotify for instance), which have limited the phenomenon (McKenzie, 2020).

5.2.2 Effects on the Supply Side

On the supply side, the development of new technologies has changed the cost structure in all cultural industries. Traditional cultural goods production has been generally characterized by being a labour intensive process, with high variable costs, and raising salaries with stagnant productivity (Baumol & Bowen, 1965; 1966). In contrast, high sunk costs but low marginal costs and, in turn, significant economies of scale characterize the overall structure of cultural and creative industries in the digital era. As a result, relevant concentration processes have occurred in some cultural sectors (Baumol, 2006; Fernández-Blanco & Prieto-Rodríguez, 2020), especially in the distribution segment, leading also to a shift in the balance of power from production to distribution (Simon, 2012; De Voldere et al., 2017). Such cost reduction has been made possible by the development of DT, which have resulted in new digital commodities, namely digitized goods, the born-digital ones and the metadata (Navarrete Hernández, 2013), thus enlarging the set of those traditionally handled by cultural institutions. Digitization has different implications on production, preservation and distribution, depending on the type of cultural goods (Navarrete, 2013). In fact, when the cultural content can be almost equally expressed in a different format (such as in the cases of music or books), digitisation represents a form of conversion, otherwise it is actually a surrogacy of the original item (such as in the case of a statue) (Poole, 2010). In both cases, digitisation allows providers for supplementing the access to the original item with access to the digital one, whose cost is generally low (Waldfogel, 2020), and to set the optimal mix of different forms of access (Cavalieri et al., 2023). Furthermore, digitisation may make preservation easier, depending on the nature of the original object. In the extreme it can represent a new channel for preservation, unless the material existence of the original item has a value *per se* (Peacock & Rizzo, 2008). In any case, digitisation requires specific technical equipment for the production, storage, and provision of access to users of the digitized items, but its impact on the cost structure strictly depends on the characteristics of those items.[7] Finally, metadata favour cataloguing but may also represent a support to users if they are allowed to access them. DT have changed the way cultural institutions manage their catalogue, through the development of digital document management systems, as well as the provision of access services by combining (online and onsite) digital and physical access, and have brought a reorganisation of the production process overall (Navarrete Hernández, 2013).

DT have outdated traditional business models (Searle, 2017), and challenged established funding schemes. More specifically, DT favoured the emerging of new financial platforms that opened new funding channels, such as crowdfunding, reducing transaction costs and potentially lessening the problem of tight budget constraints and reducing the dependence from public funds in some sectors (Rizzo, 2016). Crowdfunding platforms allow for raising funds from a large number of contributors who may participate with small amounts of money in exchange for moral or physical reward (generally increasing in the amount of contribution),[8] and thus work as a selection mechanism for potential cultural goods directly based on consumers' preferences (Giardina et al., 2016). In this sense, it has been claimed that crowdfunding democratizes the process of funding cultural and creative products but may also threaten public support to arts and culture (Brabham, 2017).

New technologies also indirectly affected cultural institutions, through improving financial services, namely with the development of online payment tools (Cicchiello et al., 2023). In fact, online payment systems make transactions easier and cheaper, but also resolve an information asymmetry to the extent to which they allow for recording transaction history, thus working in favour of small operators (in cultural industries as much as in other industries), which generally bear larger credit risks (Cicchiello et al., 2023).

5.2.3 Effects on the Demand Side

On the demand side, DT have changed consumption patterns in qualitative and quantitative terms (Rizzo, 2016), to the extent that DT lowered the cost of cultural consumption and stimulated the diffusion of new consumption possibilities, new types of cultural experience, and new cultural preferences (Potts, 2014). The diffusion of the Internet has created a new channel of consumption, namely online access to digitized goods, thus enhancing the dissemination of culture (Baumol, 2006) although with differences among groups and institutions, (i.e., the so-called digital divide problem) and among types of institutions.[9] Moreover, new digital commodities changed consumption habits and generally led to increased consumption of cultural goods (Waldfogel, 2020).

The increase in the supply of (digital) products, jointly with that of digital pieces of information (including the metadata made available), has enlarged the sources of information available to users, allowing them to partially avoid traditional intermediaries and to exploit the opportunity to access items remotely or physically, onsite or online. Thus, two problems have emerged for cultural institutions, with different relevance and implications depending on their type. First, the potential weakening of the role of (some) gatekeepers of culture. Second, the potential substitutability between physical and digital access (Navarrete Hernández, 2013; Cavalieri et al., 2023).

Moreover, DT further weakened the traditional distinctions among producers and consumers possibly overcoming the concept of *prosumerism* (Kotler, 1986) towards the one of *active cultural participation* (Sacco et al., 2018). Such shift in the relationship between users and cultural content has been made possible as the production of content became easy and affordable (Manovich, 2009). Producer and user are nowadays interchanging roles within a socially pervasive context, where production, passive use and creative reuse overlap even without market mediation (Sacco et al., 2018). Such processes have significantly boosted cultural capital accumulation by spurring the acquisition of cultural skill needed to actively participate with creative process.

Some scholars have also argued that DT have changed the nature of some commodities, moving them from private towards public goods by weakening their characteristics of rivalry and excludability (Salaün, 2013; Benhamou, 2015; Guccio et al., 2016). In fact, DT may affect both the characteristics of cultural goods, when existing items can be duplicated in a digital version or newborn-digital goods can be created. Implications of such phenomenon varies with the types of items and providing institutions.

5.2.4   *Effects of the Covid-19 Pandemic*

The Covid-19 pandemic has sped up the above trends. Online access to cultural commodities has been the only available channel for a relatively long period, thus leading providers to improve online services, pushing out of the market those who were unable to catch-up in the implementation of new technologies. Although after the Covid lockdown period traditional channels of consumption partially resumed, online access has established itself as an emerging and increasing way of consumption of several types of cultural commodities. However, in the very next months after lockdown, new legal requirements, such as those restricting the number of users allowed on site, further expelled from the market the suppliers (movie theatres, especially) who could not adapt for structural reasons, and anyway put additional pressure on those remaining in (Smith, 2020).

5.3   Diffusion of DT among Public Libraries

As said, the introduction of DT in libraries and, among them, of Internet-based ones traces back to at least the early 1990s (McClure et al., 1994; Bertot, 2009) if not earlier (Gasaway, 2010). Bertot (2009) shows that the share of US public libraries providing public access Internet connectivity was around 20 percent in the mid-nineties and grew fast in the following years, to almost the 99 percent at the beginning of the twenty-first century. However, worldwide, the share of libraries with Internet access is remarkably lower (around 28%) and even lower for community and school libraries (4%, and 8%, respectively).[10]

In the United States, library collections have increased due to the spread of digital collections that in 2019 accounted for more than the 50 percent of total collection (Rizzo, 2022).[11] The composition of the collections has changed remarkably in the last decade. E-books represent overall 35 percent, thus almost equalling books (39%), while audio and video have increased very much in the period. Such changes have impacted costs, which have seen a remarkable increase in the period, driven by digital collections. However, the cost per item decreased by 40 percent, notwithstanding the increase in the average cost per book (+10%).

As for Europe, according to the Enumerate Core Survey[12] (Europeana, 2017), the 87 percent of surveyed libraries has a digital collection or is engaged in digitization projects, while this share is lower for all the other types of surveyed cultural institutions.

However, remarkable differences exist among types of libraries regarding technology.[13] In common with film institutes and broadcasting archives, a large share of national libraries (94%) and academic ones (77%) possess born-digital collections. In contrast, this share is 52 percent for public libraries, similarly with museums (Europeana, 2017). Such heterogeneity reflects the functions of the different types of libraries (as well as the variety in the types of items collected) and, in turn confirms that libraries cannot be treated as a single homogeneous type of institutions.

Digitisation of preserved collections by cultural institutions has been strongly supported in Western countries through several programs. Nonetheless, the most updated data available show a slow pace in such a process (Europeana, 2017) for all cultural institutions in Europe,[14] with libraries showing the lowest share of already digitized items, and roughly half of the collections still to be digitized.

However, digitisation cannot spur any benefit to users unless digital information has been made available for online access. With this perspective, libraries (followed by archives) are by far headliners, as 78 percent of them provide the metadata online (while the percentage is around 33% for museums) and 58 percent provide online access to digitally reproduced or born digital content (against the 32% of archives and the 28% of museums). Libraries also show a higher percentage (94%) of accessible digital objects, more than any other type of institution (the 74% of all digital objects is available online and, the 20% is accessible offline). Other figures show that in general libraries are forerunners with respect to DT application to the purpose of providing access (Europeana, 2017).

Libraries declare they spend on average the 24 percent of their structural annual costs in archiving activities, and 19 percent in webservers, websites, and mobile facilities maintenance. The acquisition of digital-born material weights for the 24 percent of incidental costs. Such values are in line with other institutions. Focusing on preservation activity, only 29 percent of libraries have a written digital strategy on long-term digital preservation, against an average value of 27 percent in the Enumerate sample. Such value hides marked differences among types, probably reflecting the different types of collected items and different missions. In fact, the percentage is remarkably higher for national libraries (65%, against 66% of national archives that show the highest percentage) than for academic libraries (31%), public libraries (25%) and other types (23%).

5.4 DT and the Supply of Public Libraries' Services

5.4.1 Effects on Libraries' Functions

From a supply-side perspective, on the one side DT have been a tool to improve, enlarge and diversify the provided services, including the acquisition of books, cataloguing, interlibrary loan, publishing, delivery, access provision and internal administration (Kinney, 2010; Salaün, 2013), and thus has represented an opportunity to set the role of public libraries in a changing world (D'Elia, 2002; Gasaway, 2010; Copeland & Barreau, 2011; Elkin, 2011; Halpin et al., 2015). On the other side, DT can be seen as a threat for public libraries, to the extent that DT transforms services and products, extending collections to digital products that require new management models and policies (Tavares et al., 2018; Obi, 2023). This implies tailored training programs for library staff, and threaten public libraries' traditional functions (Copeland & Barreau, 2011; Obi, 2023).

First of all, DT have introduced new roles and functions for public libraries and changed the existing ones (Copeland & Barreau, 2011). Thanks to the spread of technologies, public libraries, and especially academic ones, are now Internet access providers (Bertot, 2009; Cancro, 2016; Kouper, 2016), which has allowed them to play a relevant role in bridging the digital divide (Muddiman et al., 2000; Kenny, 2010). Also, public libraries have gained the roles of content producers, providers of e-government services, digital workplace/space, and digital information literacy training programs (Higgs et al., 2013; Cohron, 2015; Leguina et al., 2021; Rizzo, 2022), among others (Kenny, 2010). Also, new born-digital products have been developed, some of them overcoming the traditional distinctions among cultural goods (e.g. audio-books), while e-books have had a significant impact on the book industry overall (Benhamou, 2015).[15] Finally, technologies have allowed public libraries to expand and enrich their services to enlarge the audience and to better serve the local communities (Copeland & Barreau, 2011) through the provision of information, literacy programs (Eisenberg et al., 2008) and the creation of digital collections of local significance (Dalbello, 2004). New roles have come partially at expense of traditional roles, according to some scholars (McClure & Jaeger, 2009; Rizzo, 2022) and have anyway changed, and probably increased, workloads for librarians (Kenny, 2010; Cloonan, 1993). In fact, a critical aspect for libraries nowadays has to do with the required technical knowledges and skill that library workers need to have for libraries to fully exploit the potential of DT and respond to new needs of visitors and users (Bryant and Poustie, 2001; Bertot, 2009; Kaun and Forsam, 2022; Ashiq et al., 2022).

DT have had a massive and multifaceted impact on preservation. Theoretically, digitisation and online access have served the purposes of improving preservation by making the digital copy only available to users. In fact, they have added further tasks to libraries to the extent to which digitisation of material items does not prevent the need for preserving the latter, while it generates the problem of preserving their digital copies (Cloonan, 1993; Obi, 2023). The problem of conserving material items refers to the durability of the material they are made of and requires librarians to improve conditions of storage and use. Clearly this problem remains for libraries nowadays, though it may be reduced shifting the use from the physical item to the digital one, and is extended to the need for maintaining the supports of digital items, such as computers, drives, and so forth. However, the main aspect of digital items preservation concerns obsolescence of the formats in which knowledge is stored. In fact, digital formats have proven to be subject to obsolescence relatively quickly, thus digitisation requires libraries to plan an ongoing process of copying and conversion from one format to a new one (Cloonan, 1993), subject to the continuous emerging and falling of standards (Copeland & Barreau, 2011). Also, the definition of the appropriate format depends on the purpose. In fact, the best format for providing long-term use and access is not necessarily the best for current use and transfer (Copeland & Barreau, 2011). An additional problem has to do with whether to keep preserving media in obsolete formats, as not all the features of a media can be perfectly replicated from one format to a new one.[16] All the above aspects imply that nowadays libraries have to supplement the traditional task of preserving a material item from physical deterioration with the task of preserving pieces of information and knowledge, stored in different formats with the respective operative problems (Cloonan, 1993; Schwartz, 2000).

DT can help cultural institutions store information easily and at a lower cost than in the past (Obi, 2023) but this brings up additional problems such as those related to security management and protection from manipulation (Cloonan, 1983; Gasaway, 2010; Copeland & Barreau, 2011; Obi, 2023).[17] This aspect is particularly relevant for libraries although it affects also other cultural institutions. On the one hand, ensuring that stored pieces of information would not be altered by anyone is key to the function of preserving knowledge for future generations. On the other hand, protection of stored data is necessary to avoid data breaches, especially when it comes to sensitive or confidential information (Chowdhury, 2014; Obi, 2023). For both issues, librarians have been required to develop effective security management protocols (Vavousis et al., 2020; Obi, 2023).[18]

5.4.2 Market Effects

The relatively low cost of producing, storing, and providing digital content (Benhamou, 2015), opens up room to new providers. Theoretically this feature affects public cultural institutions less than private ones, to the extent to which public ones are not meant to compete with private providers but to supply access to the public-owned heritage and preserve knowledge for future generations. However, it is unlikely that the fast growth of new providers and new content may come at no cost for cultural institutions such as national libraries, who are often meant to collect and preserve the whole supply of cultural content available in the field (Larivière, 2001), which, in fact increases at a faster rate than in the past. Public libraries also have had the function of filtering the supply of knowledge, choosing which items deserved to be preserved and made available for access, but the spread of new markets have determined a process of disintermediation between users and providers (publishers and libraries) (Benhamou, 2015).

Furthermore, the classification and indexing of the collection allows users to easily search among items and within them. This is what

Salaün (2013) calls the opportunity gain of libraries. Such functions and services have been fulfilled by public libraries as monopolists for a long time, due to the costs connected to storage and duplication of books but, nowadays, private Web search engines compete with public libraries.

A further issue regards the relationship between libraries and one of their most relevant counterparts, namely the publishers. Long before the digital revolution, the establishment of the book industry had substituted libraries in one of their traditional functions, that is, knowledge production. DT have allowed publishers to improve and enlarge their supply. Many publishers nowadays supply online access to a large range of journals and publications, either directly or through libraries under license. A process of concentration in the book industry has led to the presence of a few large publishers, whose market power with respect to libraries has grown significantly, allowing them to keep licences' price high and to include contractual clauses that prevent the use of legitimately-accessed material (IFLA, 2022), thus providing more and more pressure on libraries (Salaün, 2013; IFLA, 2022). However, recent editorial models, such as the Open Access option have partially weakened the market power of publishers, but to the advantage of Internet giants such as Amazon and Google (Benhamou, 2015) more than that of public libraries. According to some authors, the low cost of production, storage, preservation and access provision of digital content is expected to dramatically change the way such functions have been exercised so far.[19]

5.4.3 Financial Effects

More in general, DT diffusion, in a context of increasingly binding budget constraints, has challenged the financial sustainability of libraries (Borin & Donato, 2023) due to the direct and indirect costs of digitisation, including the initial investments (Chowdhury, 2014) and those regarding the internal organisation and staff training. Indeed, the needed investments have changed the cost structure of libraries (Europeana, 2017) and even brought libraries to have a dedicated budget or to seek external funding, mainly through Friends of Library Groups (Bertot, 2009), sometimes exploiting new methods for fundraising, including crowdfunding, which is however still a residual source (Europeana, 2017) or, eventually, for some types of libraries, the sale of the digital copies of specific valuable items in their collection. For, instance, historical libraries or those with a specialized collection, may follow different strategies regarding the digital copies in relation to their aims and to the historical and artistic importance of the item, the type of user and the quality of the copy, with different implications in terms of raising revenue.[20]

Jointly with financial issues, new emerging commodities and the presence of alternative providers for similar services in some cases at a tiny, or no, cost (especially on the Internet) severely challenge libraries' organisation and provision, especially in the case of public libraries that may have less flexibility in undertaking major transformations.

5.4.4 Digital Libraries

The spread of digital content and, in parallel, of electronic resources (e-books, and e-journals' articles, especially) have enlarged the set of products collected by public libraries and created a new type of libraries, namely digital libraries. This concept may refer to different types of providers of library services (Schwartz, 2000). First, it may refer to libraries collecting and providing digital items that are accessed mainly (if not only) remotely. This is the result of an ongoing pro- cess of evolution of libraries that continuously follows technological innovation by integrating new technologies in the provision of library services (Gasaway, 2010).[21] While all types of libraries have started to collect and provide digital content, digital libraries are of specific relevance for academic (Joo & Lee, 2011) and school (Elkin, 2011) libraries. For them, the provision of new born-digital goods, such as multimedia and audiovisual, besides e-books, has been recognized to be especially important (Joo & Lee, 2011) in the face of competi- tion with other emerging sources of information easily available on the Internet (Gasaway, 2010; Elkin, 2011). Clearly, such evolution brought up the problem of developing new business models in the industry (Houghton et al., 2010) including those related to e-books and e-journal subscriptions and open access protocols (Chowdhury, 2014).

In a different sense, the concept of digital libraries refers to the result of a process of convergence among different types of cultural institutions, which has become possible thanks to DT (Schwartz, 2000). Starting in the mid-1990s, a wide range of (mainly) public initiatives at national or international levels have created unique portals that provide access to the knowledge preserved by libraries, archives, museums, and so forth. Such digital libraries are in fact funded either by governments or specific consortia (Chowdhury, 2014).[22] The reason why such initiatives have grown in number in the last year is that they provide quick and easy access across a wide range of types of items in electronic format (Schwartz, 2000).

However, the provision of access to digital items brings up several critical issues for libraries. One of them regards property rights in the digital environment. Copying and access provision are generally subject to licensing agreements, which have become more complex due to the enhanced possibilities of access brought up by technologies. Licensing agreements may in fact include access restrictions, limiting for instance the number of accesses at one time (or the access to specific groups of users), and further problems come from the possibility to disassemble the digital item into parts (Schwartz, 2000).

Finally, most recent technologies – only partially exploited so far – such as artificial intelligence, have shown impressive potential and in the next few years are expected to change, even more, the context in which public libraries operate (IFLA, 2017; Li et al., 2019).[23]

5.4.5 The Covid-19 Pandemic and the Supply of Public Libraries

An already considerable number of studies have tackled this issue, trying to study how and to what extent the pandemic has forced library services to adapt to a context wherein the traditional channel of service delivery, namely the onsite provision, had become temporarily unusable (Ashiq et al., 2022), and the demand for digital content dramatically increased (Borin & Donato, 2023). The need for maintaining the service operative for an unpredictable period had compelled libraries to suddenly enhance online provision and thus to exploit and extend the use of DT (Gòmez-Zapata et al., 2023), notwithstanding the lack of teleworking culture and digital skills of workers and of sufficient technological infrastructures (Tammaro, 2020; Ćirić & Ćirić, 2021; Ashiq et al., 2022). In such a context, public libraries also had to enhance their use of social media and websites to reach remote users.[24]

Specifically, the lockdown paused the process of digitization,[25] as librarians started working remotely from home and because of copyright clauses (Tammaro, 2020), and forced libraries to enhance remote access of the existing digital materials (Ćirić and Ćirić, 2021). The pandemic led publishers to offer expanded access to their items, that is, at a lower cost, but for a limited period, so that libraries did not manage to expand their offer meaningfully (IFLA, 2022). Also, legal issues emerged with respect to online education, with regard to the use of copyrighted content and recording (IFLA, 2022).[26] The following partial lockdown allowed a resumption of the digitization while onsite lending and borrowing was very limited and performed through home delivery (Tamaro, 2020) due to the legal restrictions in terms of distancing and number of users allowed on site (Smith, 2020). Therefore, in this period, digital access development was complemented by digitization tasks (Ćirić and Ćirić, 2021).

The pandemic generally increased cooperation among libraries, especially through interlibrary loan and with other institutions (Tammaro, 2020), and enforced the implementation of digital services (Smith, 2020). Also, in the countries and in the periods in which public libraries have been among the few institutions open to the public, they have played the role of crucial social infrastructure, providing additional services, well beyond their traditional functions (Ashiq et al., 2022; Kaun & Forsman, 2022).

5.5 DT and the Demand for Public Libraries' Services

Equally to other cultural institutions, the diffusion of DT has changed the way and the extent to which individuals demand library services. A new channel of consumption, namely Internet, has allowed easy access to digital content and represents an additional opportunity or a threat for libraries (Aabo, 2005; Rankin & Brock, 2012). In fact, DT have enlarged the audience of libraries that have initiated remote access but, on the other hand, the demand for library services may be reduced because of the enlargement of leisure opportunities and of new sources of information and knowledge, especially for young people (Elkin, 2011; Rankin & Brock, 2012).[27]

Digitization weakens the characteristics of private goods of books when they are copied or directly produced in the digital format (e-books). In fact, once in the digital format, the book is not fully *rival* anymore,[28] as more individuals may read the book simultaneously, even accessing the same file. Also, it is not fully *excludable*, as limiting the access to those who pay for it, though still possible, requires sophisticate technologies, thus being more expensive. Thus, digital copying may weaken the excludability of the item in the long term. At least, the extremely low cost of duplication makes the book easily accessible by more and more readers, thus allowing for increasing their consumption. The diffusion of e-books and creation of the respective market have received little attention in the economic literature (Benhamou,

2015), though their increasing dynamics has been remarkable in the last decades. The significant price gap between a book and the respective e-book may displace the consumption of material books, this effect depending, however, on existing regulation.[29] But it may also affect the demand for library services, depending on contractual agreement between publishers and libraries. Figures show that in some countries (especially in northern Europe), e-loans may in future cannibalize e-sales (De Voldere et al., 2017). Thus, analogous to the supply side, the effect of DT on the demand for library services is theoretically ambiguous, and this topic has attracted the interests of scholars in several fields. The main issue regarding the relationship between libraries and DT refers to whether libraries and Internet are complement or substitute.[30] The Internet has presented a new channel for accessing a broad range of commodities, including cultural products such as books, and provides a public space for the development, exchange, and spread of ideas and knowledge. Given that the digital revolution is far from being over and the use of the Internet keeps increasing around the globe, if the Internet is, among other things, a substitute for libraries, public libraries may not have a future (Aabø, 2005). In the last decades, such an issue has been studied extensively, above all in the library Information Science literature, with mixed results. While several scholars have suggested that the spread of the Internet, especially, and of DT as a whole, would have displaced libraries, representing a threat for them (Li, 2008), other authors have found evidence of a complementarity (D'Elia et al., 2002), arguing that technologies would have increased the scope of libraries bringing new users and, thus, new value for public libraries. However, Wyatt et al. (2015) and Rizzo (2022) show that the number of registered members has remained stable or even increased notwithstanding the reduction of the number of circulating physical items, and of visits, suggesting that new services compensate the reduction of the traditional services provided, also attracting non-traditional library users.

Users may find it preferable to access the digital copy than the physical one because of its digital features – for instance for the possibility to easily search the whole text (Gasaway, 2010). Digital books and articles can be used more easily than traditional books, providing that people can access them. Compared to other digital products, the potential for use is even larger, given their relatively small size, and their fast-increasing quantity due to the low cost of production (Copeland & Barreau, 2011).

In fact, the demand for e-books and articles has increased in the last decade (Benhamou, 2015; Rizzo, 2022) and even more during the Covid-19 pandemic (Tammaro, 2020; Ćirić and Ćirić, 2021). In parallel, the use of mobile devices increased at the expense of personal computers (Ćirić and Ćirić 2021; Rizzo, 2022). However, as already discussed, technologies have opened room for new providers of services, such as, for instance, web search engines to find information to the detriment of search services provided by libraries (Salaün, 2013). Such phenomena are not neutral, as web search engines use algorithms that are driven by for-profit concerns, in contrast to libraries, so that the shift of search activities from them to the Web should be analysed also in terms of possibly lower social capital accumulation.

Similarly to the supply side, the potential of DT from the demand side has been limited so far, specifically due to the very well-known issue of digital divide (Jaeger et al., 2012). Unless access to technologies is spread among groups, only a part of the society can benefit from it, with the consequence of making disparities even harsher, given that the digital divide hits disadvantaged people (Wyatt et al., 2015). On this point, public libraries have played an equalizing role so far, partially bridging the digital divide to the extent that digitally disadvantaged individuals have exploited the opportunity to access library computers (Kinney, 2010; Quick et al., 2013; Rizzo, 2022). To fully exploit such opportunity, public libraries need to be accessible to the whole population, and specifically to marginalized groups (Muddiman et al., 2000; Aabø, 2005; Higgs et al., 2013; Chowdhury, 2014). Nevertheless, digital divide does not refer only to the possibility to access the Internet, but also to the possession of the required skills to fully exploit the potential of access. Empirical evidence shows that even after removing barriers to access, inequalities in skills persist (Leguina et al., 2021).

Notes

1   See Sacco et al. (2018) for a discussion on this point.
2   Examples of such policies and projects at national level are 'Digital First with the User in Mind' in Sweden; 'digital-made-in.de', and the Deutsche 'Digitale Bibliothek' (German Digital Library) in Germany; the 'Digital Library Initiatives' in USA, the 'Finnish Library Act (1998)' in Finland and so forth. At the EU level, it is worth noting the 'Digital Preservation Europe (EU)', the Europeana iniative and the recent European Collaborative Cloud for Cultural heritage – ECCCH (Borin & Donato, 2023).

3 See for instance Black & Pepper (2012) for a history of public libraries in Britain.

4 Salaün (2013) shows how DT have increased the power of editors of scientific journals at the expense of libraries.

5 More information about IFLA trends and the trend reports can be found at: https://trends.ifla.org/.

6 Theoretically, piracy may stimulate sales, but many empirical evidences support the displacement hypothesis. See McKenzie (2020) for a comprehensive literature review on this topic.

7 Such requirements are in fact relatively less demanding for libraries than for museums, for instance, given that the digitisation of a publication is less costly than producing a 3D replication of a statue or a building.

8 On the diverse types of crowdfunding and their effects, see OECD (2022).

9 The tools to provide online access clearly varies with the type of digital item, and thus with the type of institution. For instance, 3D tools for providing virtual visits have been almost exclusively implemented in museums.

10 Our elaboration on data provided on the IFLA LMW website.

11 Physical items accounted for 98 percent of total collections in 2009 (Rizzo, 2022).

12 The Enumerate Core Survey offers, among others, data on digital engagement of European cultural institutions. About a thousand institutions responded, on a voluntary basis, to the 2017 wave of the survey, including a very wide range of entities. The participation rate to the survey strongly varies across countries and types of institutions and, thus, data are not fully representative of the entire population.

13 As for Italy, Tammaro (2020) reports that academic libraries have substantially invested in the acquisition of licenses to enhance digital provision but generally kept the organization of workflows developed for printed books.

14 Such a trend is likely to change as consequence of the NextGenerationEU plan, including in its priorities the promotion of digital transition,

15 See Section 5.5 for the main issues regarding e-books in libraries provision.

16 For instance, the specific features of an LP cannot be replicated when the audible item has been replicated to a digital format. The same applies to books as well. Depending also on people preferences, traditional format can be considered not replicable, apart from technical issues.

17 A related issue concerns the increasing demand for big data in the digital library field (De Mauro et al., 2016; Li et al., 2019; Albergaria & Jabbour (2020). Data stored by digital libraries have the characteristics of big data, which implies the need for using appropriate security protocols. Also, big data are increasingly recognized as a key tool for digital libraries to move from resource-sharing service to a user-oriented one (Li et al., 2019).

18 DT also raise relevant ethical issues such as that of the right to be for-gotten. Such aspect is beyond the scope of this book. See Kritikos (2018) for a comprehensive discussion on this point.

19 According to Copeland & Barreau (2011), such a process may possibly lead to the disappearance of physical libraries in the long run. However, a recent study on US libraries (Rizzo, 2022) shows that while visits to libraries declined in the last decade, the number of registered borrowers as well as the size of collections have reached a maximum.

20 For instance, Bertacchini & Morando (2013) report the partnership between the Bundesarchiv and the Wikimedia Foundation, based on Creative Commons Licenses, which consisted in the release of some 100,000 images of the archive collection under an open content license to be distributed from Wikipedia, with the only requirement for users to attribute and share-alike.

21 Libraries providing online and onsite services are sometimes referred to as hybrid libraries (Schwartz, 2000).

22 The National Science Digital Library and the Digital Library Initiatives (USA), Internet Culturale (ITA), as well as the already mentioned Europeana and the German Digital Library are among the most relevant examples of digital libraries as repository of items preserved by different institutions, involving members ranging from archives to museums and libraries.

23 Although such a family of technologies has generally affected all indus-tries, an increasing strand of literature addresses the current and potential impact of artificial intelligence on library supply. See Subaveerapandiyan (2023) for a review of studies on this topic.

24 However, in some countries during the pandemic, public libraries were recognized as crucial social infrastructure and consequently remained open to the public, as a free space providing Internet connectivity (Kaun & Forsman, 2022).

25 Public libraries in some cases tried without success to obtain exceptions to copyright agreements so as to be allowed to digitize textbooks (Tammaro, 2020).

26 Technical and legal restrictions on streaming platforms, sharing and recording had affected libraries indirectly, by compensating the increase in the demand of their online services, but also directly, either because licenses limited to on site access were not re-negotiated, or because of differences in copyright laws among countries, which limited the pro-vision of services to those students who returned in their own countries (IFLA, 2022).

27 See Chapters 2 and 4 on this point.

28 According to Salaün (2013) material books for loan in libraries are them-selves not pure rival goods, as lending is generally limited to a specific period so as to allow others to enjoy the book.

29 In France, for instance, the regulation of resale price, implying a fixed book price, applies also to e-books (Benhamou, 2015).
30 From an economic point of view, two commodities are substitute when the consumption of one of them reduces the other commodity's consumption. Similarly, two commodities are complement if the consumption level of one increases when individuals increase the consumption of the other.

References

Aabø, S. (2005). The role and value of public libraries in the age of digital technologies. *Journal of Librarianship and Information Science*, 37(4), 205–211. https://doi.org/10.1177/0961000605057855

Albergaria, M., & Jabbour, C. J. C. (2020). The role of big data analytics capabilities (BDAC) in understanding the challenges of service information and operations management in the sharing economy: Evidence of peer effects in libraries. *International Journal of Information Management*, 51. https://doi.org/10.1016/j.ijinfomgt.2019.10.008

Ashiq, M., Jabeen, F., & Mahmood, K. (2022). Transformation of libraries during Covid-19 pandemic: A systematic review. *Journal of Academic Librarianship*, 48(4). https://doi.org/10.1016/j.acalib.2022.102534

Baumol, W. J., & Bowen, W. G. (1965). On the performing arts: The anatomy of their economic problems. *American Economic Review*, 55(1/2), 495–502. www.jstor.org/stable/1816292

Baumol, W. J., & Bowen, W. G. (1966). *Performing Arts. The economic dilemma. A study of problems common to theater, opera, music and dance.* New York: The Twentieth Century Fund.

Baumol, W. J. (2006). The arts in the "New Economy". In Ginsburg, V. A. & Throsby, D. (Eds.). *Handbook on the economics of art and culture*, Vol. 1. Amsterdam: Elsevier, 339–358.

Benhamou, F. (2015). Fair use and fair competition for digitized cultural goods: The case of eBooks. *Journal of Cultural Economics*, 39, 123–131. https://doi.org/10.1007/s10824-015-9241-x

Bertacchini, E., & Morando, F. (2013). The future of museums in the digital age: New models of access and use of digital collections. *International Journal of Arts Management*, 15(2), 60–72. https://www.jstor.org/stable/24587113

Bertot, J. C. (2009). Public access technologies in public libraries: Effects and implications. *Information Technology and Libraries*, 28(2), 81–91. https://doi.org/10.6017/ital.v28i2.3176

Black, A., & Pepper, S. (2012). From civic place to digital space: The design of public libraries in Britain from past to present. *Library Trends*, 61(2), 440–470. https://doi.org/10.1353/lib.2012.0042

Borin, E., & Donato, F. (2023). Financial sustainability of digitizing cultural heritage: The International Platform Europeana. *Journal of Risk and Financial Management*, 16(10), 421. https://doi.org/10.3390/jrfm16100421

Brabham, D. C. (2017). How crowd funding discourse threatens public arts. *New Media & Society*, 19(7), 983–999. https://doi.org/10.1177/146144481 5625946

Bryant, J., & Poustie, K. (2001). *Competencies needed by public library staff.* Gutersloh: Bertelsmann Foundation.

Cancro, P. (2016). The dark (ish) side of digitization: Information equity and the digital divide. *The Serials Librarian*, 71(1), 57–62. https://doi.org/10.1080/0361526X.2016.1157424

Cavalieri, M, Ferrante, L, Martorana, M. F., & Rizzo, I. (2023). The ICT strategy of Italian museums: Institutional, supply and demand side drivers. *Economics of Innovation and New Technology*, 1–21. https://doi.org/10.1080/10438599.2023.2222268

Chowdhury, G. (2014). Sustainability of digital libraries: A conceptual model and a research framework. *International Journal on Digital Libraries*, 14, 181–195. https://doi.org/10.1007/s00799-014-0116-0

Cicchiello, A. F., Gallo, S., & Monferrà, S. (2023). Financing the cultural and creative industries through crowdfunding: The role of national cultural dimensions and policies. *Journal of Cultural Economics*, 47(1), 133–175. https://doi.org/10.1007/s10824-022-09452-9

Cichocki, K. M. (2007). Unlocking the future of public libraries: Digital licensing that preserves access. *University of Baltimore Intellectual Property Law Journal*, 16(1–2), 29–59.

Ćirić, J., & Ćirić, A. (2021). The impact of the COVID-19 pandemic on digital library usage: A public library case study. *Journal of Web Librarianship*, 15(2), 53–68. https://doi.org/10.1080/19322909.2021.1913465

Cloonan M. V. (1993). The preservation of knowledge, *Library Trends*, 41(4), 594–605.

Cohron, M. (2015). The continuing digital divide in the United States. *The Serials Librarian*, 69(1), 77–86. https://doi.org/10.1080/03615 26X.2015.1036195

Copeland, A. J., & Barreau, D. (2011). Helping people to manage and share their digital information: A role for public libraries. *Library Trends*, 59(4), 637–649. DOI: 10.1353/lib.2011.0016

Dalbello, M. (2004). Institutional shaping of cultural memory: Digital library as environment for textual transmission. *Library Quarterly*, 74(3), 265–298. https://doi.org/10.1086/422774

D'Elia, G., Jörgensen, C., Woelfel, J., & Rodger, E. J. (2002). The impact of the Internet on public library use: An analysis of the current consumer market for library and Internet services. *Journal of the American Society for Information Science and Technology*, 53(10), 802–820. https://doi.org/10.1002/asi.10102

De Mauro, A., Greco, M., & Grimaldi, M. (2016). A formal definition of Big Data based on its essential features. *Library Review*, 65(3), 122–135. https://doi.org/10.1108/LR-06-2015-0061

De Voldere, I., Romainville, J. F., Knotter, S., Durinck, E., Engin, E., Le Gall, A., Kern, P., Airaghi, E., Pletosu, T, Ranaivoson H., & Hoelck, K. (2017). *Mapping the creative value chains a study on the economy of culture in the digital age. Final Report.* European Commission. www.open-heritage.eu/wp-content/uploads/2020/12/mapping-the-creative-value-chain.pdf

Eisenberg, M., Lowe, C., & Spitzer. K. (2008). Information literacy: Essential skills for the information age. *DESIDOC Journal of Library & Information Technology*, 28(2), 39–47. http://dx.doi.org/10.14429/djlit.28.2.166

Elkin, J. (2011). The user of tomorrow: Young people and the future of library provision. In Evans, W. & Baker, D. (Eds.) *Libraries and society: Role, responsibility and future in an age of change*, Chandos Publishing, 235–251.

Europeana (2017). *D.4.4 Report on ENUMERATE Core Survey 4.* https://pro.europeana.eu/files/Europeana_Professional/Projects/Project_list/ENUMERATE/deliverables/DSI-2_Deliverable%20D4.4_Europeana_Report%20on%20ENUMERATE%20Core%20Survey%204.pdf

Fernández-Blanco, V., & Prieto-Rodríguez, J. (2020). Cost of production. In Towse, R. & Navarrete Hernández, T. (Eds.). *Handbook of cultural economics*, 3rd ed., Cheltenham: Edward Elgar Publishing, 129–136.

Gasaway, L. N. (2010). Libraries, digital content, and copyright. *Vanderbilt Journal of Entertainment & Technology Law*, 12(4), 755–778.

Giardina, E., Mazza, I., Pignataro, G., & Rizzo, I. (2016). Voluntary provision of public goods and technology. *International Advances in Economic Research*, 22, 321–332. https://doi.org/10.1007/s11294-016-9582-z

Gómez-Zapata, J. D., Herrera-Moreno, M. A., & Herrero-Prieto, L. C. (2023). Valuing cultural public goods in times of pandemic: What happened to the libraries? *Journal of Librarianship and Information Science*, 1–79. https://doi.org/10.1177/09610006231196345

Guccio, C., Martorana, M. F., Mazza, I., & Rizzo, I. (2016). Technology and public access to cultural heritage: The Italian experience on IT for public historical archives. In Borowiecki, K. J., Forbes, N. & Fresa, A. (Eds.) *Cultural heritage in a changing world*. Heidelberg: Springer, 55–76.

Halpin, E., Rankin, C., Chapman, E. L., & Walker, C. (2015). Measuring the value of public libraries in the digital age: What the power people need to know. *Journal of Librarianship and Information Science*, 47(1), 30–42. https://doi.org/10.1177/0961000613497746

Higgs, G., Langford, M., & Fry, R. (2013). Investigating variations in the provision of digital services in public libraries using network-based GIS models. *Library & Information Science Research*, 35(1), 24–32. https://doi.org/10.1016/j.lisr.2012.09.002

Houghton, J. W., & Oppenheim, C. (2010). The economic implications of alternative publishing models. *Prometheus*, 28(1), 41–54.

IFLA (2017). *Advances in artificial intelligence.* https://trends.ifla.org/literature-review/advances-in-artificial-intelligence

IFLA (2021). *Trend Report 2021 Update*. https://repository.ifla.org/handle/123456789/1830

IFLA (2022). *How well did copyright laws serve libraries during COVID-19? Research Report*. https://repository.ifla.org/handle/123456789/1925

Jaeger, P. T., Bertot, J. C., Thompson, K. M., Katz, S. M., & DeCoster, E. J. (2012). Digital divides, digital literacy, digital inclusion, and public libraries. *Public Library Quarterly*, 31(1), 1–20. http://dx.doi.org/10.1080/01616846.2012.654728

Joo, S., & Yeon Lee, J. (2011). Measuring the usability of academic digital libraries: Instrument development and validation. *The Electronic Library*, 29(4), 523–537. https://doi.org/10.1108/02640471111156777

Kaun, A., & Forsman, M. (2022). Digital care work at public libraries: Making digital first possible. *New Media & Society*. https://doi.org/10.1177/14614448221104234.

Kinney, B. (2010). The internet, public libraries, and the digital divide. *Public Library Quarterly*, 29(2), 104–161. https://doi.org/10.1080/01616841003779718

Kotler, P. (1986). Prosumers: A new type of consumer. *The Futurist*, 20, 24–28.

Kouper, I. (2016). Professional participation in digital curation. *Library & Information Science Research*, 38(3), 212–223. https://doi.org/10.1016/j.lisr.2016.08.009

Kritikos, K. C. (2018). Delisting and ethics in the library: Anticipating the future of librarianship in a world that forgets. *IFLA Journal*, 44(3), 183–194. https://doi.org/10.1177/0340035218773783

Larivière, J. (2001). *Guidelines for legal deposit legislation*. UNESCO. https://unesdoc.unesco.org/ark:/48223/pf0000121413

Leguina, A., Mihelj, S., & Downey, J. (2021). Public libraries as reserves of cultural and digital capital: Addressing inequality through digitalization. *Library & Information Science Research*, 43(3), 1–9. https://doi.org/10.1016/j.lisr.2021.101103

Li, B. (2008). *American libraries and the Internet: The social construction of web appropriation and use*. Youngstown, NY: Cambria Press.

Li, S., Jiao, F., Zhang, Y., & Xu, X. (2019). Problems and changes in digital libraries in the age of big data from the perspective of user services. *Journal of Academic Librarianship*, 45(1), 22–30. https://doi.org/10.1016/j.acalib.2018.11.012

Manovich, L. (2009). The practice of everyday (media) life: From mass consumption to mass cultural production?. *Critical Inquiry*, 35(2), 319–331. https://doi.org/10.1086/596645

McClure, C. R., Bertot, J. C., & Zweizig, D. (1994). *Public libraries and the Internet: Study results, policy issues, and recommendations*. Washington, DC: US National Commission on Libraries and Information Science.

McClure, C. R., & Jaeger, P. T. (2009). *Public libraries and Internet service roles: Measuring and maximizing Internet services.* Chicago: American Library Association.

McKenzie, J. (2020). Digital piracy. In Towse, R. & Navarrete Hernández, T. (Eds.). *Handbook of cultural economics*, 3rd ed., Cheltenham: Edward Elgar Publishing, 228–234.

Michnik, K. (2015). Public libraries digital services and sustainability issues. *The Bottom Line*, 28(1/2), 34–43. https://doi.org/10.1108/BL-12-2014-0034

Muddiman, D., Durrani, S., Dutch, M., Linley, R., Pateman, J., & Vincent, J. (2000). *Open to all? The public library and social exclusion*, Vol. 1. London: The Council for Museums, Archives and Libraries.

Navarrete Hernández, T. (2013). Digital cultural heritage. In Rizzo, I. & Mignosa, A. (Eds.) *Handbook on the economics of cultural heritage*, Cheltenham, UK: Edward Elgar Publishing, 251–271.

Noh, Y. (2011). Evaluation of the resource utilization efficiency of university libraries using DEA techniques and a proposal of alternative evaluation variables. *Library Hi Tech*, 29(4), 697–724. https://doi.org/10.1108/073788 31111189787

Obi, H. E. (2023). Prevalence of digitization and security management in archives preservation in public libraries in Rivers state. *American Journal of Science on Integration and Human Development*, 1(1), 55–66.

OECD (2022). The culture fix. Creative people, places and industries. *Local Economic and Employment Development (LEED)*. Paris: OECD Publishing. https://doi.org/10.1787/991bb520-en

Peacock, A., & Rizzo, I. (2008). *The heritage game: Economics, policy, and practice*. Oxford: OUP.

Poole, N. (2010). The *cost of digitizing* Europe's *cultural heritage, a report for the Comité des Sages of the European Commission*, http://ec.europa.eu/ information_society/activities/digital_libraries/doc/reflection_group/anne xes/digitisation-final-report.pdf

Potts, J. (2014). New technologies and cultural consumption. In Ginsburg, V. A. & Throsby, D. (Eds.) *Handbook of the economics of art and culture*, Vol. 2. Elsevier, 215–231.

Quick, S., Prior, G., Toombs, B., Taylor, L., & Currenti, R. (2013). *Cross-European survey to measure users' perceptions of the benefits of ICT in public libraries*. Final Report. TNS (funded by the Bill and Melinda Gates foundation). https://digital.lib.washington.edu/researchworks/handle/ 1773/22718

Rankin, C., & Brock, A. (2012). Library services for children and young people: An overview of current provision, future trends and challenges. In Rankin, C. (Ed.) *Library services for children and young people–an overview of current provision, future trends and challenges*. London: Facet, 3–27.

Rizzo, I. (2016). Technological perspectives for cultural heritage. In Rizzo, I. & Towse, R. (Eds.) *The Artful Economist: A New Look at Cultural Economics*, Cham: Springer, 197–214.

Rizzo, N. (2022). State of US public libraries–more popular & digital than ever. *WordsRated*, February, 17. https://wordsrated.com/state-of-us-public-libraries/

Sacco, P. L., Ferilli, G., & Tavano Blessi, G. (2018). From culture 1.0 to culture 3.0: Three socio-technical regimes of social and economic value creation through culture, and their impact on European Cohesion Policies. *Sustainability*, 10(11), 1–23. https://doi.org/10.3390/su10113923

Salaün, J. M. (2013). The immeasurable economics of libraries. In Rizzo, I. & Mignosa, A. (Eds.) *Handbook on the economics of cultural heritage*, Cheltenham, UK: Edward Elgar Publishing, 290–306.

Schwartz, C. (2000). Digital libraries: An overview. *Journal of Academic Librarianship*, 26(6), 385–393. https://doi.org/10.1016/S0099-1333(00)00159-2

Searle, N. (2017). Business models, intellectual property and the creative industries: a meta-analysis. *Create Working Paper 2017/09*.

Shim, W. (2003). Applying DEA technique to library evaluation in academic research libraries. *Library Trends*, 51(3), 312–332.

Shim, W., & Kantor, P. B. (1998). A novel economic approach to the evaluation of academic research libraries. *Proceedings of the Annual Meeting-American Society for Information Science*, 35, 400–410.

Simon J. P. (2012). *The dynamics of the media and content industry: A synthesis*. JRC Technical Reports. http://ipts.jrc.ec.europa.eu

Smith, J. (2020). Information in crisis: Analysing the future roles of public libraries during and post-COVID-19. *Journal of the Australian Library and Information Association*, 69(4), 422–429. https://doi.org/10.1080/24750158.2020.1840719

Subaveerapandiyan, A. (2023). Application of Artificial Intelligence (AI) In libraries and its impact on library operations review. *Library Philosophy and Practice*, (e-journal), 7828, 1–19. https://digitalcommons.unl.edu/libphilprac/7828

Tammaro, A. M. (2020). COVID 19 and libraries in Italy. *International Information & Library Review*, 52(3), 216–220. https://doi.org/10.1080/10572317.2020.1785172

Tavares, R. S., Drumond, G. M., Angulo Meza, L., & Mexas, M. P. (2018). Efficiency assessment in university libraries. *Transinformação*, 30, 65–79. https://doi.org/10.1590/2318-08892018

Vavousis, K., Papadopoulos, M., Polley, J., & Xenakis, C. (2020). A compliant and secure IT infrastructure for the National Library of Greece in consideration of internet security and GDPR. *Qualitative and Quantitative Methods in Libraries*, 9(2), 219–236.

Waldfogel, J. (2020). Digitization in the cultural industries. In Towse, R. & Navarrete Hernández, T. (Eds.). *Handbook of Cultural Economics*, 3rd ed., Cheltenham: Edward Elgar Publishing, 235–240.

Wyatt, D., McQuire, S., & Butt, D. (2015). *Public libraries in a digital culture*. Melbourne: University of Melbourne.

6 Conclusions

Libraries are widely spread cultural institutions that can be considered part of any urban landscape. What a library is and what its mission is are not trivial issues. In fact, libraries are quite heterogeneous entities with broad and diversified objectives that have gradually modified their functions through time in relation to societal evolution, adapting also to cultural and technological changes.

Different types of libraries interact with society in different ways, depending on the specific functions. The provision of knowledge and culture has been joined through time with services to support people, with marked attention to social inclusion and the accumulation of social and cultural capital. The library's role in society and its positive contribution to the economy provide strong motivation for public support at different levels of government. However, governmental action does not necessarily ensure the fulfilment of society's wellbeing. Indeed, the features of the institutional framework matter, bringing about a different set of incentives on librarians and, more in general, on libraries' staffs. Hence, there is a need for evidence-based public decisions, with a useful role played by valuation, both at a micro level, regarding the performance of libraries, and at macro level, to ensure that resources are allocated to produce value for money.

The diversified characteristics and role of the different types of libraries call for tailored policies, notwithstanding the importance of government support to all of them. The sustainability of local and community libraries, which sometimes may be the only cultural 'garrison' in small villages, requires public resources as well as people support and engagement, the latter being, however affected by the availability of public funding, and by the ability of the library's staff to meet society's needs. The weight of additional resources,

DOI: 10.4324/9781003331896-6

deriving from the services sold, is likely to be negligible for small local libraries, while it can be important for big ones located in urban contexts, especially if they have valuable collections and/or are hosted sometimes in outstanding buildings. These libraries may also rely on various forms of private support, though the implication for the public nature of libraries needs to be taken into account. The capability to meet the sustainability challenges, diversifying the sources of income, is however affected by the legal and administrative framework, which impacts the incentives provided to the library staff. A supply-oriented approach, disregarding users' preferences, may lead to libraries' underutilization and may limit cultural participation, with a negative impact on the overall benefits generated.

In general, as data show, public participation in libraries raises important issues. Indeed, participation varies widely across countries, as it is shown in Europe, probably related to the features and the size of public intervention, and it is generally lower than for other cultural institutions. Though, this appears somehow in contrast with the positive appreciation of the public as assessed by several valuation studies worldwide, a possible explanation being the relevance of non-use values. Being library services characterized by positive externalities to cultural and social capital accumulation, with positive implications for society's wellbeing, public policies are called for to enhance cultural participation. The integration of libraries within the overall supply of cultural events and a strategy to diversify activities to meet the needs of different segments of users might prove to be an effective means. In such a perspective, special attention might be paid to children and, more in general, to young generations who have more potentialities in terms of cultural capital accumulation.

Libraries also have shown to be able to face several challenges over time, the most recent and pervasive example being the digital revolution. Notwithstanding the challenges deriving from the digital revolution, libraries still have a crucial role in the formation of human capital and, as gate-keepers of knowledge: even though such a monopolistic function does not hold anymore, libraries have maintained their function of distribution of knowledge and an intermediating role, though in competition with other actors. This raises two different issues. On the one hand, changes in the market structure driven by the diffusion of digital technologies, favouring concentration at production and distribution level, tend to weaken the contractual power of libraries, with potentially severe consequences in terms of financial sustainability. On the other hand, it may result in a partial shifting to the private sector of the decision on what to preserve for current and future generations and to provide for them, thus undermining the fulfilment of public objectives. Furthermore, the shift of search activities from libraries to new providers, such as Web search engines, should be analysed also in terms of possibly lower social capital accumulation, given that they use algorithms that are driven by for-profit concerns, in contrast to libraries where the filtering is usually based on expertise. This problem may be particularly relevant as long as it may impact on students' achievements whenever students' search for knowledge takes place outside the libraries' channel – online or onsite – partially displacing the function of academic libraries.

Notwithstanding threats and challenges, libraries have been able to combine traditional services, such as the loan of books, with the digital ones as well as with a wide array of activities aimed at making them a meeting place, creating social capital and, in some cases, offering support service to a diversified target of users. Indeed, their contribution to society is strengthened as long as libraries are able to reduce inequalities tackling also the digital divide and this appears to occur in advanced and in emerging economies, as well as in difficult situations, as with the recent pandemic emergency. However, these effects cannot be taken for granted, and to fully exploit the potential of libraries, the role of policies is crucial. Clear objectives, adequate incentives, and effective monitoring systems are essential steps to drive the allocation of public resources so the result is the improvement of society's wellbeing. At the same time, people engagement and public awareness are necessary ingredients for two reasons: they foster the accountability of public decision makers and institutions, and are crucial actors for the achievement of public goals.

Index

academic libraries *see* types of
  libraries
access 5, 8–9, 11–13, 26, 35–6,
  43–4, 59–61, 69–70, 76, 84–9,
  91–9; accessibility 10–11;
  barriers to 59, 73, 76, 99;
  digital access 8, 87–8, 97;
  online access 87–92, 94, 99–100;
  on-site access 87–8, 101
accessibility *see* access
active participation *see* cultural
  participation
activities 90; acquisitions/additions/
  collecting 7, 36, 43, 46–9, 91,
  100; ancillary services 35–7,
  43, 51; cataloguing 36, 40, 87,
  91; conservation/preservation/
  restoration 7, 10, 13, 35–6,
  40–1, 44, 52, 84, 86–7, 91–2,
  94; digital preservation 91–2;
  digital provision 23, 41, 66,
  96, 100–1, 109; educational
  activities 69; interlibrary loan 5,
  45, 47–8, 91, 97; lending 7–8,
  47, 77, 97, 101; onsite services
  96–7, 101, 111; referencing 7;
  search 99, 111
additions *see* activities
admission fees *see* funding
ancillary services *see* activities
archives 1–2, 10–11, 26, 35–6, 42,
  58, 72, 76, 90–1, 101
artificial intelligence 13, 96, 101

Arts Council of England 11, 15, 23
asymmetric information *see*
  information

bandwagon effect 69
barriers to access *see* access
Baumol's cost disease 41, 86
benefit/cost ratio *see* valuation
  methods
bequest values *see* non-use values
born-digital goods *see* digital goods
business models 3, 85, 87, 95

capital *see* production inputs
cataloguing *see* activities
choice experiment (CE) *see*
  valuation methods
collection 5, 7–8, 10, 20–2, 26, 36,
  40–1, 89–90; digital collection
  22, 26, 35, 89–90, 92; historical
  collection 20–1; physical
  collection 22, 35; specialized
  collection 10, 13, 95
community libraries *see* types of
  libraries
connectivity *see* Internet
conservation *see* activities
contingent valuation (CV) *see*
  valuation methods
co-production *see* production
  process
copyright 86, 96, 97, 101;
  digital piracy 86

For Product Safety Concerns and Information please contact our EU
representative GPSR@taylorandfrancis.com
Taylor & Francis Verlag GmbH, Kaufingerstraße 24, 80331 München, Germany

www.ingramcontent.com/pod-product-compliance
Ingram Content Group UK Ltd.
Pitfield, Milton Keynes, MK11 3LW, UK
UKHW021822240425
457818UK00006B/44